Water and Sanitation in Uganda

A WORLD BANK STUDY

Water and Sanitation in Uganda

Clarence Tsimpo and Quentin Wodon, Editors

WORLD BANK GROUP

Contents

Figures

Maps

Tables

Acknowledgments

This study is part of a series on service delivery and poverty in Uganda. The editors are, respectively, with the Poverty and Education Global Practices at the World Bank. The research benefitted from funding from the Technical and Administrative Support Unit (TASU) under the Joint Budget Support Framework (JBSF), as well as the Water and Sanitation Program at the World Bank. The opinions expressed in the study are those of the individual author chapters only and need not represent those of the World Bank, its executive directors, or the countries they represent. The editors are especially grateful to Ahmadou Moustapha Ndiaye (formerly country manager for Uganda), Jean-Pascal Nganou (senior economist and task manager for the TASU work program), Pablo Fajnzylber (Practice Manager, Poverty), Marlon Lezama (Senior Program Coordinator, TASU), Harry Patrinos (Practice Manager, Education), Albert Zeufack (Practice Manager, Macroeconomics), Glenn Pearce-Oroz (principal regional team leader for water and sanitation in the Africa Region), and Samuel Mutono (senior water and sanitation specialist) for guidance and support in order to complete this work. The editors are also grateful to Prospere Backiny-Yetna and Berina Uwimbabazi, who served as peer reviewers. The last chapter of the study is adapted from a separate study entitled *Water and Sanitation for the Poor and Bottom 40 Percent in Uganda: A Review of Strategy and Practice Since 2006.*

About the Editors

Clarence Tsimpo Nkengne is a Senior Economist in the Poverty Global Practice at the World Bank. Previously, he served as Economist for TASU based in Kampala, Uganda. Before joining the Bank, he worked for the National Direction of Statistics and National Accounts in Cameroon as Department Head for data bank management. He has also worked as a consultant for the Canadian Centre of International Development and Cooperation. He holds graduate degrees in statistics, economics, and computer sciences, and is finalizing a PhD in Economics from the University of Montreal.

Quentin Wodon is a Lead Economist in the Human Development Network at the World Bank. Previously, he served as Lead Poverty Specialist for Africa and as Economist/Senior Economist for Latin America. Before joining the Bank, he worked as Assistant Brand Manager for Procter & Gamble, volunteer corps member with ATD Fourth World, and Assistant Professor of Economics at the University of Namur. He holds graduate degrees in business engineering, economics, and philosophy (Université Catholique de Louvain), and PhDs in Economics (American University) and Theology and Religious Studies (Catholic University of America). Over the past two decades, Quentin's work has focused on improving policies for poverty reduction, mostly in the areas of education and health, social protection/labor, infrastructure, public finance, gender, and climate change.

Executive Summary

This study provides a basic diagnostic of access to safe water and sanitation in Uganda and their relationship with poverty. While the analysis is not meant to lead directly to policy recommendations, some of the findings are relevant for policy. The analysis relies on a series of nationally representative household surveys for the period 2002–13, as well as on qualitative data collection. The study first analyzes trends in access to safe water and some of the constraints faced by households in this area using mostly household survey data (chapter 2). The issue of the cost of water for households without a connection to the water network is discussed with a focus on public stand pipes (chapter 3). Qualitative data are then presented on the obstacles faced by households in accessing safe water (chapter 4). The last two chapters are devoted to sanitation. As for safe water, the focus is first on household survey data about sanitation, including with respect to toilets, bathrooms, waste disposal, and hand washing (chapter 5), and next on an analysis of qualitative data from focus groups and key informants (chapter 6). Finally, the study reviews policies and programs that have been implemented in order to provide access to water and sanitation for the poor, as well as options going forward (chapter 7).

The main findings are as follows:

1. Only a small minority of households has access to piped water, but under usual definitions, three in four households have access to an improved water source. Constraints to access to safe water include cost, as well as distances to safe water sources and perceptions that open water sources may be good enough. The issue of the functionality of the infrastructure is also highlighted as an issue in communities.
2. Despite a reduced price per cubic meter charged by utilities, prices for end users can be higher at public taps than for households connected to the water network.
3. Factors that contribute to a lack of availability of safe water in communities include lack of functionality (facilities are not working properly), lack of local responsibility (poor leadership hinders investments to improve water supply or leads to poor maintenance), and water scarcity (in some communities, water is simply not easily available).

4. Most households and communities are well aware of what constitutes safe water and how to keep water sources safe, but the pressure of daily life and common practices come in the way. Affordability constraints and cultural factors and attitudes are both at fault.

5. Only a small minority of households have access to improved sanitation as commonly defined, and the availability of toilets, waste disposal mechanisms, bathroom facilities, as well as hand-washing practices have not changed fundamentally over the last decade.

6. As for safe water, constraints to adequate sanitation include cultural norms and traditional behavior as well as lack of income, but poor terrain or soil type and a lack of land also play a role. In some cases, cultural traditions also lead to inadequate sanitation. When public latrines are available, there is often a consensus on fees to ensure maintenance, but enforcement is weak. The same is true for byelaws requiring households to build their own latrines.

7. While most communities and households are again aware of what should be done for waste removal, some of the same constraints are at work to limit the ability to properly dispose of waste. Hand washing remains an exception, due in part to cost and affordability, but in this case also in large part because of lack of knowledge.

Overall, the constraints faced by households are complex, often requiring solutions that must be context- and community specific. This does not lead to cookie-cutter solutions, but is important to document precisely because of the variety of local circumstances.

Abbreviations

CBMS   Community-Based Maintenance System
CBO   community-based organization
CPI   consumer price index
DDHS   District Directorate of Health Services
DEA   Directorate of Environmental Affairs, MWE
DESO   District Education and Sports Office
DWD   Directorate of Water Development, MWE
DWO   district water office/officer
DWRM   Directorate of Water Resources Management, MWE
DWSCG   District Water and Sanitation Conditional Grant
GIZ   Deutsche Gesellschaft für Internationale Zusammenarbeit (German development assistance agency)
GPOBA   Global Partnership for Output-Based Aid
GTZ   German development assistance agency, before reorganization as GIZ
IDAMC   Internally Delegated Area Management Contract (NWSC)
IFC   International Finance Corporation
ILRI   International Livestock Research Institute
JBSF   Joint Budget Support Framework
JMP   WHO-UNICEF Joint Monitoring Program for Water and Sanitation
KfW   Kreditanstalt für Wiederaufbau (lending agency of German development cooperation)
LC   local council (the levels are designated by number; for example, LC5 = District Council, Kampala City Council Authority)
MDGs   Millennium Development Goals (of the United Nations)
M&E   monitoring and evaluation
MOES   Ministry of Education and Sports
MOFPED   Ministry of Finance, Planning, and Economic Development
MOH   Ministry of Health
MWE   Ministry of Water and the Environment

MWLE	Ministry of Water, Lands, and Environment (ministry before reorganization as MWE)
NDP	national development plan
NGO	nongovernmental organization
NWSC	National Water and Sewerage Corporation
OBA	output-based aid
OECD	Organisation for Economic Co-operation and Development
O&M	operation and maintenance
PAF	Poverty Action Fund
PEAP	Poverty Eradication Action Plan
PPP	purchasing power parity
PWP	public water point
RGC	Rural growth center
RUWASS	Reform of Water Supply and Sanitation Project
RWH	rainwater harvesting
RWSSD	Rural Water Supply and Sanitation Department, DWD, MWE
SDGs	Sustainable Development Goals (of the United Nations)
SIP	Sector Investment Plan (predecessor to SSIP)
SSIP	Strategic Sector Investment Plan
SWAp	sector-wide approach
SWGs	sector working groups
TASU	Technical and Administrative Support Unit
TSU	Technical Support Unit, RWSSD, DWD, MWE
UBOS	Uganda Bureau of Statistics
UN	United Nations
UNHS	UBOS Uganda National Household Survey, various years
UOWS	Umbrella Organizations for Water and Sanitation
USD	United States dollar
U Sh	Ugandan shilling
UWSSD	Urban Water Supply and Sewerage Department, DWD, MWE
VIP	ventilated improved pit (latrine)
WASH	water, sanitation, and hygiene
WfP	Water for Production
WfPD	Water for Production Department, DWD, MWE
WHO	World Health Organization
WSDF	Water and Sanitation Development Facility (also used to refer to WSDF branch offices under UWSSD, DWD, MWE)
WSP	Water and Sanitation Program
WSSB	Water Supply and Sanitation Board

CHAPTER 1

Introduction

Clarence Tsimpo and Quentin Wodon

Access to safe water and sanitation has long been an integral part of the Ugandan Government's National Development Plan which includes references to the link between safe water, adequate sanitation, and poverty reduction. Access to safe water and sanitation play a key role in the development of the economy, with large impacts on health outcomes and time use and thereby productivity, among others. The objective of this study is to provide a basic diagnostic from the point of view of households of access (or the lack thereof) to safe water and adequate sanitation and the constraints encountered by households for such access. For the most part, the study does not focus on residential piped water, most of which is provided by the National Water and Sewerage Corporation in large cities. This is because issues related to the demand for and supply of residential piped water are covered in another study by the editors.

The present study is based on data from nationally representative household surveys and qualitative fieldwork. It consists of six chapters. After this introduction, the first three chapters (Part 1 of the study) are devoted to issues of access to safe water. Chapter 2 provides a basic diagnostic of access to improved water sources in Uganda on the basis of four rounds of nationally representative household surveys, as well as a brief quantitative analysis of focus group data. Summary statistics are provided first on trends in access to water according to detailed modalities available in survey questionnaires and then using more aggregated definitions adopted by the Joint Monitoring Programme (JMP) for water and sanitation of the World Health Organization. Constraints to access to safe water are discussed relying on both the household and community modules of existing surveys. Finally, qualitative data from focus groups on constraints faced by households are analyzed to provide a better understanding of some of the factors that limit access to safe water in communities.

The data suggest that only a small minority of households have access to piped water, whether in the dwelling or through public standpipes. When considering other water sources considered as improved by the JMP, about three in four households could have access to improved water sources, at least in principle. This proportion is slightly higher in the last two rounds of the Uganda National Household Survey than in the first two rounds. In terms of constraints for access to safe water, cost plays a role, especially in Kampala. In other areas, distances to safe water sources and perceptions that open water sources are good enough are also at play. Community leaders confirm that water is not always affordable for some households, and the issue of the functionality of the infrastructure is also highlighted as an issue in communities.

Chapter 3 discusses the issue of the cost of water for households that are not connected to the water network. When households are not connected to the water network and are forced to rely on water providers, as is typically the case in urban areas, they may end up paying a higher price per unit of consumption than households that benefit from a connection to the network. This is typically the case not only for tankers and street vendors, but also for public taps (or stand-pipes) because of the role played by intermediaries in operating the taps. In other words, even though the water at public taps may be provided at a lower price by utilities than that charged to residential customers connected to the network, the price for end users may be higher because of the operating costs and profits reaped by (often private) tap operators. The chapter first documents the sources of water used by households, noting that most households and especially the poor do not have domestic water connections. The chapter then measures the cost of water from public taps in Uganda and compares it with the cost of other sources of water. The results indicate that despite the reduced priced per cubic meter charged by utilities, the prices for end users are higher at the taps than the prices paid by residential customers directly connected to the network.

Chapter 4 complements the quantitative analysis of access (or the lack thereof) to safe water provided in chapters 2 and 3 with a detailed qualitative analysis based on focus groups and key informants interviews implemented in 14 districts. The focus is on some of the challenges and constraints faced by households in accessing safe water—as well as their ongoing efforts to improve water sources in their communities. After a brief description of the methodology adopted for the fieldwork, the presentation of the data collected is organized along two thematic issues—the availability of water in communities and the quality of the water that is available.

The factors that contribute to a lack of availability of water in many communities are analyzed along three dimensions: lack of functionality, lack of responsibility, and scarcity. Lack of functionality refers to the fact that in many communities existing water facilities are not working properly, whether this is due to (among others) aging systems, poor maintenance, or the inability to implement necessary repairs to broken down equipment because of affordability or other constraints. Lack of local responsibility refers to poor organization or leadership at the local level that prevents communities from making necessary investments in improving water supply and leads to poor maintenance and a lack of incentives for households to keep water sources clean. Scarcity of water refers to the fact that in some communities, water is simply not easily available—it is scarce and often has to be brought into the community from distant sources. All three factors play a role in reducing the access to safe water for households.

Factors that contribute to a lack of quality of the water used by households and communities are analyzed along two dimensions—the focus is first on the perceptions of what constitutes safe water, and then on factors that lead households not to take necessary steps that would improve water quality. Regarding perceptions, most households and communities are well aware of what constitutes safe water. They recognize that boiling water may be needed to ensure safety. There is also wide recognition of the need to build latrines sufficiently far away from water sources. At the same time, the pressures of daily life and common practices come in the way, because of both affordability constraints and cultural factors. As an example of affordability constraints, buying charcoal or firewood to boil water may be too costly for some households. Lack of affordability is also related to the opportunity cost in terms of time of fetching water that may be safer, but located farther away from household dwellings. As for cultural factors, in some areas perceptions that the population used to be fine in terms of health outcomes without having to protect its water sources may now lead to suboptimal outcomes when contamination risks have increased substantially because of population growth and other factors. For others, there may be a perception that if water looks clean, it can (erroneously) be assumed to be safe.

The last two chapters (part 2 of the study) are devoted to sanitation. As done for safe water in chapter 2, the analysis starts in chapter 5 with a basic diagnostic of sanitation based on nationally representative household surveys, along with a brief quantitative analysis of focus-group data. The data suggest that only a small minority of households have access to improved sanitation as defined by the JMP. The landscape of the types of toilets, waste disposal techniques, bathroom facilities, and hand washing practices observed has not changed fundamentally over the last decade. Constraints to access to sanitation are identified in the surveys, as well as in the qualitative data. Cultural traditions and traditional behaviors, negative attitudes, and lack of income are among the main reasons for incomplete latrine/toilet coverage in communities. Poor landscape or terrain, poor soil type, and a lack of land also play a role. Poor hygiene habits are also related to lack of affordability, attitudes, at times ignorance or at least cultural norms and traditional behaviors (in rural areas), and lack of space (in urban areas).

Chapter 6 then complements the quantitative analysis of chapter 5 with a more detailed qualitative analysis of some of the challenges and constraints faced by households in benefitting from adequate sanitation—as well as their ongoing efforts to improve sanitation in their dwellings and communities. The presentation of the data collected is organized along seven topics—the lack of latrines in many household dwellings, the community alternatives to private latrines, the obstacles encountered in building latrines, the incentives that can lead to building more and better latrines, the modes of waste disposal used by households, and the issue of hand washing.

The qualitative fieldwork suggests that many communities have limited toilet facilities, with quite a few of the latrines built in a state of disrepair, especially for public facilities. Private latrines are not affordable for many. Yet, apart from the cost, other obstacles including poor soil quality, lack of land rights, tenant status, and even cultural traditions all may come in the way of better sanitation. Alternatives to public or private latrines are many, but they are often inadequate. When public latrines are available, there is often a consensus that in order to ensure proper maintenance, fees should be charged to those using the latrines, yet enforcing the fees requires leadership in the community that is at times lacking. The same is true for byelaws stating, especially in urban areas, that households should build their own latrines; often enforcement of these laws is weak. Information campaigns can help in building consensus at the local level of the need for better sanitation. Some communities condition access to government programs on having a proper latrine in the home. In some areas, home inspections are organized to certify the presence of latrines. Even shaming has been used in some communities to incentivize households to build proper latrines. Technological alternatives such as Eco-San toilets have also been proposed, but these are often not seen favorably by households, and also fall in disrepair.

Beyond latrines, improved sanitation requires proper waste removal. Most communities and households are again well aware of what should in principle be done, but some of the same constraints are at work to limit the ability of households to properly dispose of waste. When local governments do not have specific regulations, households may simply do what is convenient for them. In cities, garbage disposal is in principle, but not necessarily in practice, better organized. Burning is often not allowed because of fire risks and pollution, but enforcement may be limited. As for latrines, sensitization and information campaigns can help, and when some households do not practice sound waste management, the community can retaliate using some of the same mechanisms as those mentioned in the case of latrines, but this again requires leadership.

A special focus is placed on the practice of hand washing, which remains an exception. The issue of cost and lack of affordability is again prevalent in the respondents' feedback, for example to buy necessary containers and soap—some of which may be stolen at public (or even private) facilities that do not have tight oversight. But in this specific case, lack of knowledge about the benefits of hand washing seems to be a larger issue. In one community, the threat of a cholera outbreak led members to wash hands for a while, but the practice dried up soon after.

Overall, in the case of both water and sanitation, the survey data as well as the qualitative fieldwork suggest that the constraints faced by households are complex, often requiring solutions that must be context- and community specific. This does not lead to cookie-cutter solutions, but is important to document precisely because of the variety of local circumstances.

Finally, the last chapter of the study (chapter 7 in part 3) complements the diagnostic of previous chapters by analyzing trends in public funding for the water and sanitation sector and some of the main initiatives implemented over the last decade in order to better serve the poor. The analysis suggests that public funding for the sector has increased in real terms but remains low in comparison to needs. Even though some of the schemes implemented under the 2006 pro-poor strategy have been successful, access remains low and rural households remain at a disadvantage versus urban dwellers. It is important to take stock of what has been achieved, and what remains to be done to improve access and affordability for the poor.

PART 1

Safe Water

CHAPTER 2

Access to Improved Water Sources: Quantitative Analysis

Clarence Tsimpo and Quentin Wodon

Introduction

This chapter provides a basic diagnostic of access to improved water sources in Uganda on the basis of nationally representative household surveys, as well as a quantitative analysis of focus group data. Summary statistics are first provided on trends in access to water according to detailed modalities available in survey questionnaires and more aggregated definitions adopted by the Joint Monitoring Programme (JMP) for water and sanitation of the World Health Organization. Constraints to access to safe water are then discussed relying on both the household and community modules of existing surveys. Finally, qualitative data on constraints faced by households are analyzed to provide a better understanding of some of the factors that limit access to safe water in communities.

Improved water sources as well as adequate sanitation are essential for a range of development outcomes, including the reduction of diarrheal deaths and malnutrition among young children, who are especially vulnerable to waterborne diseases. Access to safe water and sanitation reduce infant and child mortality, morbidity, and malnutrition (on those links, see among many others Esrey et al. 1991; Esrey 1996; Kosek, Bern, and Guerrant 2003; Jalan and Ravallion 2003; Dillingham and Guerrant 2004; Fay et al. 2005; Hutton and Haller 2004; Moe and Rheingans 2006; Zwane and Kremer 2007; Bhutta, Ahmet, and Black 2008; Cairncross, Hunt, and Boisson 2010; World Bank 2010; Alderman et al. 2013; and Spears 2013). Several millions people die from diarrheal diseases every year, and most of these deaths can be attributed to unsafe water supply, poor sanitation, and poor hygiene conditions. As a result, access to clean water could reduce diarrhea and waterborne diseases by 25 percent (Schuster-Waller et al. 2008).

The importance of water and sanitation for health has been recognized in human rights declarations as well as in the Millennium Declaration under the seventh goal with target as the reduction by half the proportion of people without sustainable access to safe drinking water and basic sanitation by 2015. Although safe water has been provided to 1.6 billion people since 1990, another one billion people worldwide still lack access, with most living in poor countries; in Sub-Saharan Africa, two out of every five people may lack access to safe drinking water.

Providing safe water and adequate sanitation is not only the right thing to do, but it is also a sound investment for governments and donor agencies, as well as communities. In Africa and Asia, access to safe water has been shown to generate high potential benefit-to-cost ratios (Rijsberman and Zwane 2012). This is also why access to safe water and adequate sanitation are included in 25 essential interventions identified by Denboba et al. (2014) for early childhood development. In short, improved access to safe water may well be the single most cost-effective means of overcoming water-related death and disease globally (for a cost-effectiveness study applied to Uganda, see Barungi and Kasirye 2011)

Apart from generating health benefits especially for young children, access to safe water also improves the productivity of adolescents and adults by relieving household members (especially girls and women) from time-consuming water fetching (Blackden and Wodon, 2006). In most African countries, women and girls are most likely to collect water. Lack of access to safe water also has implications for the time it takes to cook, do the laundry, clean, and care for young children. Evidence shows that household cooking methods—including in terms of the type of water used which may require wood burning—have direct effect on the health of households and their related health expenditure, which again may affect productivity, income levels, and thus poverty. Walking far away from home to fetch water also places women and girls at a heightened risk of crime in some countries. Studies for Uganda (Bbaale and Buyinza, 2012) attribute part of primary school absenteeism to intra-household time use and labor substitution whereby school-age children are deployed toward fetching water and firewood.

The importance of safe water and sanitation for development is without doubt. In this context, the objective of this study, including this chapter, is to provide a basic diagnostic of access to improved water sources in Uganda, starting with an analysis of nationally representative household surveys, but including as well an analysis of focus-group qualitative data. Specifically, three complementary sources of data are used for the analysis in this chapter.

First, summary statistics on trends in access to water are provided according to the detailed modalities available in the Uganda National Household Survey questionnaires, as well as in a more aggregated way following the definitions proposed by the Joint Monitoring Programme (JMP) for water and sanitation of the World Health Organization. According to the JMP, an improved drinking-water source is one that, by the nature of its construction and when properly used, adequately protects the source from outside contamination, particularly fecal matter. Improved water sources include piped water into dwelling or yard/plot, public taps or standpipes, tube wells or boreholes, protected dug wells, protected springs, and rainwater. By contrast, unimproved water sources include unprotected springs, unprotected dug wells, carts with small tanks/drums, tanker-trucks, surface waters, and bottled water. The JMP has also introduced the concept of the drinking-water ladder, which distinguishes households relying on surface water from those using other unimproved water sources, then from those using improved sources but not piped water, and, finally, from those with network connections in their home.

Data are available in the same surveys on how far water sources are located from where households live, the time it takes for households to go to and from the sources, and the time it takes to wait at the source to get water. Finally, community leaders are asked in the community module of the surveys to assess changes in access to safe water, whether communities have undertaken activities to protect water catchment areas, and if so what type of activities.

Second, a separate panel survey that is also nationally representative provides additional useful information about why some households do not rely on safe water sources that could be available to them. That survey also provides data from community leaders on their assessment of the cost of water for households and the affordability of water for them.

Third, another way to look at constraints faced by households and communities to gain access to improved water sources consists in implementing a simple quantitative analysis of feedback received from communities through qualitative fieldwork. In chapter 4, data from this qualitative fieldwork are analyzed in details and organized along two thematic issues—the availability of water and its quality. In this chapter, part of the feedback provided by households in focus groups is visualized quantitatively on the basis of responses to a question asked to focus group participants about challenges for access to safe and clean water in communities.

The structure of the chapter is as follows. Section 2 discusses trends in access to water sources. Section 3 discusses some of the constraints faced by households and communities in their access to safe water sources. A conclusion follows.

Trends in Access to Water Sources

This section discusses trends in access to water sources using nationally representative surveys. Summary statistics from the last four rounds of the Uganda National Household Survey on sources of drinking water are provided in table 2.1. In 2012/13, despite an expansion of the networks of the National Water and Sewerage Company (NWSC) and of water utilities in smaller towns under the supervision of the Ministry of Water and Environment, only 7 percent of households had piped water in their dwelling or yard (for an analysis of piped water in Uganda, see Tsimpo and Wodon 2017). As expected, piped water coverage rates are much higher among households in the top welfare quintile than among the poor—in part because connections are concentrated in Kampala and large cities. Network connection rates are virtually inexistent in the bottom half

Table 2.1 Main Source of Drinking Water for Households

Percent

	Location			Region				Welfare quintile					Total
	Kampala	Other urban	Rural	Central	Eastern	Northern	Western	1	2	3	4	5	
2012/13													
Piped water into dwelling	11.1	4.4	0.3	3.3	1.0	0.5	1.5	0.0	0.0	0.5	0.8	5.2	1.7
Piped water to the yard	34.7	13.2	1.0	10.7	3.2	0.8	4.9	0.0	0.8	2.3	5.2	13.3	5.3
Public taps	36.1	22.3	5.3	14.3	5.3	2.8	18.5	2.9	5.0	8.0	11.7	19.2	10.6
Borehole in yard/plot	1.1	1.0	0.6	0.8	0.9	0.8	0.3	0.7	0.6	0.7	0.6	0.9	0.7
Public borehole	1.3	26.1	39.4	18.1	53.3	56.1	15.6	50.0	43.8	38.8	30.1	20.8	34.6
Protected well/spring	11.2	14.9	17.8	15.3	17.5	14.5	20.1	13.7	22.4	17.1	18.2	14.0	16.8
Unprotected well/spring	2.3	7.9	22.3	22.9	6.6	18.5	25.1	18.7	17.1	22.1	21.6	13.4	18.2
River/stream/lake	0.0	2.1	8.2	5.2	6.3	5.4	9.2	9.7	6.1	7.0	7.0	4.1	6.5
Vendor	0.6	4.5	1.1	4.7	0.7	0.0	0.9	0.2	0.4	1.1	1.7	4.2	1.8
Tanker truck	0.0	0.0	0.1	0.0	0.0	0.0	0.2	0.0	0.1	0.0	0.0	0.1	0.1
Gravity Flow Scheme	0.0	0.9	1.9	0.0	4.6	0.3	1.4	3.6	2.4	1.3	1.3	0.5	1.6
Rainwater	0.0	1.3	1.3	2.5	0.2	0.0	1.8	0.2	0.7	0.7	1.2	2.5	1.2
Bottled water	1.2	1.0	0.2	1.1	0.0	0.1	0.2	0.0	0.0	0.0	0.0	1.4	0.4
Other	0.4	0.4	0.6	0.9	0.6	0.1	0.4	0.5	0.7	0.6	0.5	0.5	0.5
Total	100.0	100.0	100.0	100.0	100.0	100.0	100.0	100.0	100.0	100.0	100.0	100.0	100.0
2009/10													
Private connection to pipeline	21.4	18.9	1.7	10.8	2.0	1.9	3.5	1.2	0.7	1.3	1.9	15.1	5.1
Public taps	59.5	40.1	5.1	24.7	6.2	4.3	12.0	3.1	6.0	6.8	14.7	25.9	13.0
Borehole	0.4	18.0	39.7	18.7	55.8	54.0	15.9	47.8	40.4	38.8	34.5	20.1	34.4
Protected well/spring	13.9	12.1	20.5	13.5	18.2	18.7	27.7	18.0	22.5	23.2	21.3	13.1	19.1
River, stream, lake, pond	1.1	3.1	26.6	22.9	11.4	19.4	35.0	26.9	27.9	24.4	21.7	14.5	22.1
Vendor/tanker truck	1.3	5.5	2.1	5.5	1.5	0.1	1.3	0.0	0.7	1.0	2.3	6.0	2.5
Gravity flow scheme	0.0	0.8	1.3	0.2	1.5	0.5	2.6	1.2	0.9	1.8	1.2	0.9	1.2
Rainwater	0.2	0.5	1.1	2.2	0.2	0.0	1.1	0.2	0.4	0.6	1.0	2.0	1.0
Other	2.3	0.9	1.7	1.5	3.2	0.9	0.8	1.6	0.6	2.0	1.4	2.4	1.7
Total	100.0	100.0	100.0	100.0	100.0	100.0	100.0	100.0	100.0	100.0	100.0	100.0	100.0

table continues next page

Table 2.1 Main Source of Drinking Water for Households (%) *(continued)*

Percent

	Location			Region				Welfare quintile					Total
	Kampala	Other urban	Rural	Central	Eastern	Northern	Western	1	2	3	4	5	
2005/06													
Private connection to pipeline	17.9	10.6	1.6	6.8	2.9	0.9	2.8	0.7	1.1	1.3	1.6	11.4	3.7
Public taps	51.2	35.0	4.8	17.9	6.0	6.1	12.2	3.7	5.8	8.3	13.5	21.1	11.4
Borehole	0.7	21.9	33.8	16.5	50.0	51.4	12.0	44.1	35.8	30.0	26.8	19.2	30.1
Protected well/spring	21.0	14.5	22.0	21.4	21.0	16.0	25.5	19.8	23.6	22.1	23.4	17.9	21.2
Unprotected well/spring	1.9	6.9	22.0	17.5	12.1	19.8	26.5	20.4	22.6	24.9	18.2	11.4	19.0
River, stream, lake, pond	0.8	2.4	11.6	12.0	5.1	4.5	15.7	9.5	9.1	10.6	11.7	8.5	9.8
Vendor/tanker truck	6.2	6.4	2.1	6.7	0.9	0.2	1.7	0.2	0.3	1.3	2.0	8.3	2.8
Gravity flow scheme	0.0	1.4	1.4	0.1	1.9	1.1	2.2	1.1	1.5	1.1	1.8	0.8	1.2
Rainwater	0.0	0.7	0.4	0.7	0.1	0.0	0.6	0.2	0.2	0.1	0.4	1.0	0.4
Other	0.4	0.3	0.4	0.4	0.1	0.2	0.8	0.3	0.1	0.3	0.7	0.4	0.4
Total	100.0	100.0	100.0	100.0	100.0	100.0	100.0	100.0	100.0	100.0	100.0	100.0	100.0
2002/03													
Tap/piped water	78.7	41.9	4.0	26.0	6.6	4.3	9.7	2.5	4.9	6.4	11.2	31.3	13.0
Borehole	0.0	22.8	31.6	20.6	44.3	37.9	14.9	35.1	28.6	31.7	26.6	23.3	28.5
Protected well/spring	13.5	18.6	22.1	16.0	17.0	28.0	26.8	20.4	24.2	22.9	23.1	16.7	21.1
Rainwater	0.0	0.4	0.4	0.5	0.0	0.4	0.7	0.3	0.4	0.2	0.4	0.6	0.4
Gravity flow scheme	0.0	2.7	4.8	1.3	4.0	0.2	11.4	2.8	4.1	5.0	6.4	3.1	4.3
Open water sources	4.1	7.2	36.0	31.2	27.4	28.8	35.6	38.0	37.2	33.0	31.0	20.4	30.8
Water truck/water vendors	3.1	6.1	0.9	4.0	0.4	0.1	0.8	0.6	0.2	0.5	1.1	4.1	1.5
Other	0.6	0.4	0.3	0.5	0.4	0.4	0.3	0.3	0.3	0.4	0.2	0.6	0.4
Total	100.0	100.0	100.0	100.0	100.0	100.0	100.0	100.0	100.0	100.0	100.0	100.0	100.0

Source: Data from UNHS surveys.

of the population in terms of welfare levels. Public taps (or standpipes), which are often run by the National Water and Sewerage Corporation, play an important role, serving a larger share (10.6 percent) of households than private connections.

Other sources of drinking water include boreholes in yards/plots, public boreholes, protected wells/springs, unprotected wells/springs, rivers/streams/lakes, water vendors, tanker trucks, gravity flow schemes, rainwater, bottled water, and other water sources. The three main water sources for households, a large majority of which lives in rural areas, are public boreholes (for 34.6 percent of households), unprotected wells/springs (18.2 percent), and protected wells/springs (16.8 percent). These are sources of water on which most of the poor rely. In addition, among the poor almost 10 percent of households rely on rivers, streams, and lakes.

While access to piped water on household premises has increased over time—almost doubling since 2005/06 when only 3.7 percent of households had private connections—this was from a low base and it did not fundamentally affect levels of access to safe water, especially as the share of households relying on public taps did not increased over time. In 2005/06, 11.4 percent of households relied on public taps versus 10.8 percent in 2012/13 (in 2002/03, the survey does not distinguished private connections from households relying on public taps).

Why are coverage rates progressing in absolute percentage points terms relatively slowly despite substantial growth in the residential customer base of NWSC in large cities and growth for other providers in small towns? As noted by Tsimpo and Wodon (2017), part of the answer comes from population growth. In 2002/03, the population in the country as measured through the weights available in the household survey for that year was at 25.2 million people.[1] In 2012/13, the population size had increased to 35.3 million people, a gain of more than a third in just one decade. But in addition, as noted by Diallo and Wodon (2007), the decrease in the average household size is also at play. In 2002/03, the average household size was 5.1, versus 4.8 in 2012/13. As a result, the number of households in the country increased more rapidly than the population, from 4.9 million households in 2002/03 to 7.1 million in 2012/13, an increase of 44 percent. Said differently, the average reduction in household size in the country over the decade is responsible for a fifth of the overall growth in the number of households, with the rest of that growth coming from population growth. Under such conditions, even rapid growth in connections from the utility companies may translate in only slow growth in coverage rates.

Unfortunately, the share of households relying on unprotected water sources which may not be safe decreased only slowly over time. In 2002/03, the proportion of households relying on open water source was at 30.8 percent. In 2005/06 and subsequent years, that category is split into two (unprotected wells/springs, and rivers, streams, lakes, and ponds), but the share of households relying on those sources is essentially the same at 28.8 percent. In 2009/10, the categories changed again, but in 2012/13, the two categories are listed, and together account still for 24.7 percent of households (18.2 for unprotected wells/springs, and 6.5 percent rivers, streams, lakes, and ponds), suggesting limited progress. For the poor, the proportion is higher.

Statistics on access to various water sources are often presented in a different and more aggregated way. While different definitions of what constitutes a safe water sources are used in the literature, it is customary to rely on the definitions proposed by the JMP for water and sanitation of the World Health Organization. As noted in the introduction, according to the JMP, an improved drinking-water source is such that the risk of outside contamination, particularly from fecal matter, is minimal. Such sources include piped water sources (piped water into dwelling or yard/plot, as well as public taps or standpipes), tube wells or boreholes, protected dug wells, and protected springs, plus rainwater. Unimproved water sources include unprotected springs, unprotected dug wells, carts with small tanks/drums, tanker trucks, surface waters, and bottled water. Apart from classifying water sources as improved or unimproved, another more detailed approach consists in considering a drinking-water ladder.

The various approaches are summarized in table 2.2 which lists the categories available in the various household surveys for Uganda used in this study according to the drinking-water ladder. Unimproved sources are at the bottom of the table and improved sources are categorized in various ladders all the way up to piped schemes, with a differentiation of whether households have piped water connections, or whether they rely on public taps or gravity flow schemes.

Table 2.3 provides statistics on access to improved and unimproved water sources following the above approach, with various subclassifications of improved sources according to the drinking-water ladder. Access to improved water sources has improved over time, but only slowly, with 72.4 percent of households in principle having access to improved water in 2012/13, versus 67.2 percent in 2002/03 (in the 2011 Demographic and Health Survey, the proportion of households with

Table 2.2 Classification of Water Sources in the Surveys According to the JMP Ladder

Questionnaire	2002/03 Survey	2005/06 Survey	2009/10 Survey	2012/13 Survey
Piped scheme	Tap/piped water	Private connection	Private connection	Piped water in the dwelling Piped water in the yard
	Gravity flow schemes	Public taps Gravity flow scheme	Public taps Gravity flow scheme	Public taps Gravity flow scheme
Borehole	Borehole	Borehole	Borehole	Borehole in yard/plot Public borehole
Other improved sources	Protected well/spring Rainw0ater	Protected well/spring Rainwater	Protected well/spring Rainwater	Protected well/spring Rainwater
Unimproved sources	Open water sources Water truck/water vendor	River/stream/lake/pond Unprotected well/spring Vendor/tanker truck	River/stream/lake/pond Vendor/tanker truck	Unprotected well/ spring River/stream/lake Vendor Tanker truck
Other sources	Other	Other	Other	Bottled water Other

Source: Background work for a World Bank Report on Water and Sanitation in Uganda (World Bank 2015).

Table 2.3 Improved Water Sources and the Drinking-Water Ladder

Percent

	Location			Region				Welfare quintile					Total
	Kampala	Other urban	Rural	Central	Eastern	Northern	Western	1	2	3	4	5	
2012/13													
Improved sources	95.4	83.7	67.5	64.7	85.8	75.9	63.9	70.8	75.4	69.2	69.0	76.2	72.4
Piped schemes	81.8	40.6	8.5	28.2	14.0	4.5	26.2	6.4	8.1	12.0	19.0	38.1	19.2
Of which on premises	45.8	17.5	1.3	14.0	4.2	1.4	6.4	0.0	0.8	2.7	6.0	18.5	7.0
Borehole	2.4	27.1	39.9	18.8	54.1	57.0	15.8	50.5	44.3	39.5	30.7	21.7	35.2
Other improved sources	11.2	16.1	19.1	17.7	17.7	14.5	21.9	13.9	23.1	17.8	19.4	16.5	18.0
Unimproved sources	2.9	14.5	31.6	32.7	13.6	23.9	35.2	28.5	23.5	30.2	30.3	21.7	26.4
Other	1.7	1.8	0.9	2.6	0.6	0.2	0.9	0.8	1.1	0.6	0.7	2.2	1.2
Total	100.0	100.0	100.0	100.0	100.0	100.0	100.0	100.0	100.0	100.0	100.0	100.0	100.0
2009/10													
Improved sources	95.1	89.9	69.4	70.0	83.8	79.5	62.6	71.4	70.5	72.6	74.4	77.0	73.7
Piped schemes	80.8	59.5	8.2	35.7	9.7	6.8	18.1	5.5	7.6	9.9	17.8	41.8	19.3
Of which on premises	21.4	18.8	1.7	10.8	2.0	1.9	3.5	1.2	0.7	1.3	1.9	15.1	5.1
Borehole	0.4	17.9	39.7	18.7	55.7	54.0	15.9	47.8	40.2	38.8	34.4	20.1	34.4
Other improved sources	14.0	12.5	21.6	15.7	18.4	18.7	28.7	18.2	22.8	23.8	22.2	15.1	20.0
Unimproved sources	2.4	8.5	28.7	28.4	12.9	19.5	36.2	26.9	28.4	25.5	24.0	20.5	24.5
Other	2.4	1.6	1.8	1.6	3.3	1.0	1.2	1.6	1.0	2.0	1.6	2.5	1.8
Total	100.0	100.0	100.0	100.0	100.0	100.0	100.0	100.0	100.0	100.0	100.0	100.0	100.0

table continues next page

Table 2.3 Improved Water Sources and the Drinking-Water Ladder (continued)

Percent

	Location			Region				Welfare quintile					
	Kampala	Other urban	Rural	Central	Eastern	Northern	Western	1	2	3	4	5	Total
2005/06													
Improved sources	90.8	84.0	64.0	63.4	81.9	75.4	55.3	69.6	67.9	63.0	67.5	71.4	68.0
Piped schemes	69.1	47.0	7.7	24.9	10.7	8.1	17.1	5.5	8.3	10.7	16.8	33.3	16.3
Of which on premises	21.4	18.8	1.7	10.8	2.0	1.9	3.5	1.2	0.7	1.3	1.9	15.1	5.1
Borehole	0.7	21.8	33.8	16.5	50.0	51.4	12.0	44.1	35.8	30.0	26.8	19.2	30.0
Other improved sources	21.0	15.2	22.5	22.1	21.2	16.0	26.1	20.0	23.8	22.2	23.8	18.9	21.7
Unimproved sources	8.9	15.7	35.6	36.2	18.1	24.4	43.9	30.1	32.0	36.7	31.8	28.1	31.6
Other	0.4	0.3	0.4	0.4	0.1	0.2	0.9	0.3	0.1	0.3	0.7	0.5	0.4
Total	100.0	100.0	100.0	100.0	100.0	100.0	100.0	100.0	100.0	100.0	100.0	100.0	100.0
2002/03													
Improved sources	92.2	86.3	62.8	64.3	71.9	70.8	63.4	61.2	61.7	66.6	67.2	75.2	67.2
Piped schemes	78.7	44.6	8.8	27.3	10.6	4.5	21.0	5.5	8.4	10.9	17.1	35.3	17.3
Borehole	0.0	22.8	31.5	20.6	44.3	37.9	14.9	34.7	29.1	31.8	27.2	22.7	28.4
Other improved source	13.5	19.0	22.5	16.5	17.0	28.4	27.5	21.0	24.3	23.9	22.9	17.2	21.5
Unimproved sources	7.2	13.3	36.8	35.1	27.7	28.8	36.4	38.4	37.9	33.0	32.7	24.1	32.4
Other	0.6	0.4	0.4	0.6	0.4	0.4	0.3	0.4	0.4	0.4	0.2	0.7	0.4
Total	100.0	100.0	100.0	100.0	100.0	100.0	100.0	100.0	100.0	100.0	100.0	100.0	100.0

Source: Estimation using UNHS surveys.

Note: In 2002/23, it is not feasible to distinguish piped water on premises or through public taps.

access to an improved water source was estimated at 70 percent; see the annex for the detailed estimates). The term "in principle" is used on purpose, because as will be shown with qualitative fieldwork in chapter 4, improved water sources are not necessarily safe or improved. In other words, progress seems to have been limited over time. Map 2.1 provides a visualization of trends in access by region over time.

Data are also available in the surveys on how far water sources are located from where households live, the time it takes for households to go to and from the sources, and the time it takes to wait at the source to actually get water. As shown in table 2.4 for 2012/13, the water sources used by households are located on average 0.8 kilometer away from their dwelling (the median is half a kilometer away), but for some households the distance is up to five kilome-

Map 2.1 Share of Households Using an Improved Water Source, 2002–13

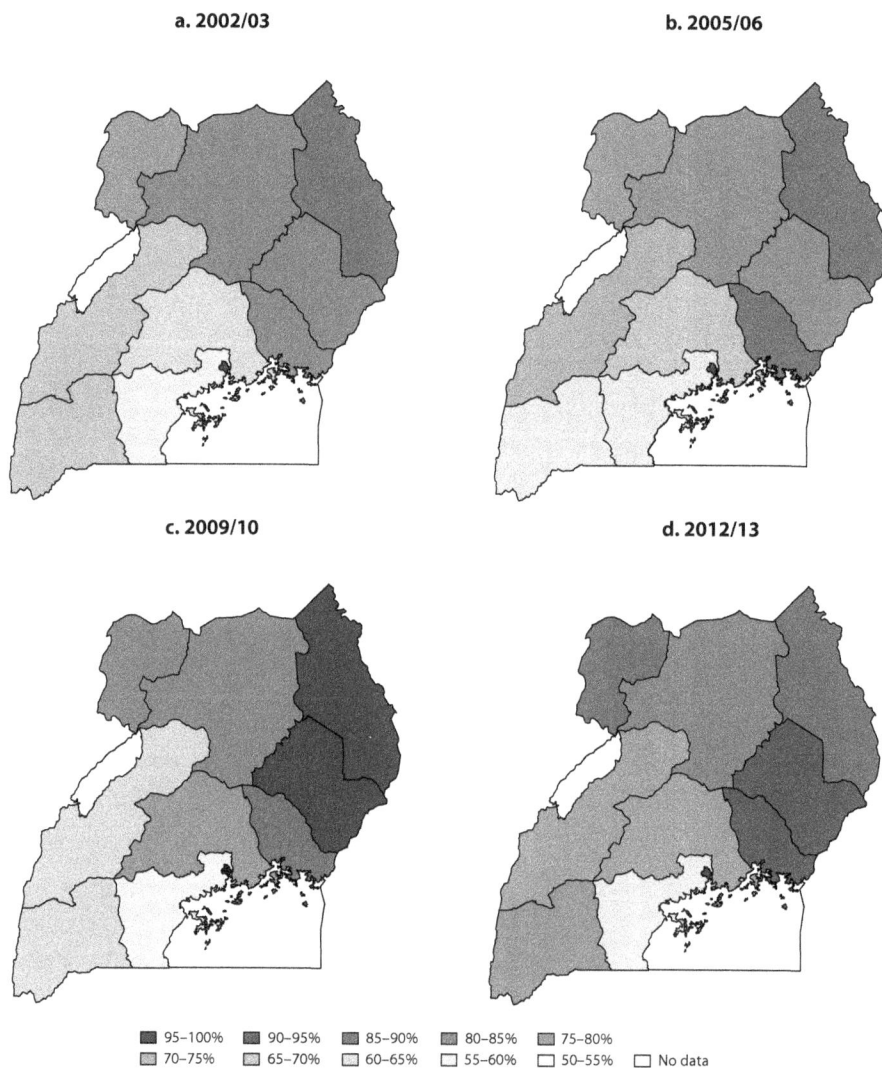

a. 2002/03

b. 2005/06

c. 2009/10

d. 2012/13

95–100% 90–95% 85–90% 80–85% 75–80%
70–75% 65–70% 60–65% 55–60% 50–55% No data

Source: Data from 2002/03, 2005/06, 2009/10, and 2012/13 UNHS surveys.

Table 2.4 Distance and Time to Drinking Water Sources for Households, 2012/13
Percent

	Residence area			Region				Welfare quintile					
	Kampala	Other town	Rural	Central	Eastern	Northern	Western	1	2	3	4	5	Total
Time to/from source (min.)													
Mean	8.9	21.3	31.5	30.8	26.2	27.5	31.4	30.1	30.5	30.1	29.4	26.2	29.0
Median	6.0	15.0	25.0	20.0	20.0	20.0	20.0	20.0	25.0	20.0	20.0	20.0	20.0
Min	0.0	0.0	0.0	0.0	0.0	0.0	0.0	0.0	0.0	0.0	0.0	0.0	0.0
Max	60.0	120.0	120.0	120.0	120.0	120.0	120.0	120.0	120.0	120.0	120.0	120.0	120.0
Waiting time at source (min.)													
Mean	7.8	20.4	22.1	13.8	27.4	31.4	13.0	25.3	25.2	22.2	20.0	17.3	21.4
Median	3.0	10.0	10.0	4.0	15.0	15.0	4.0	10.0	10.0	10.0	6.0	5.0	10.0
Min	0.0	0.0	0.0	0.0	0.0	0.0	0.0	0.0	0.0	0.0	0.0	0.0	0.0
Max	120.0	180.0	180.0	180.0	180.0	180.0	180.0	180.0	180.0	180.0	180.0	180.0	180.0
Distance from source (km)													
Mean	0.3	0.5	0.8	0.8	0.6	0.9	0.9	0.8	0.8	0.8	0.8	0.7	0.8
Median	0.1	0.3	0.5	0.4	0.4	0.5	0.5	0.5	0.5	0.5	0.5	0.4	0.5
Min	0.1	0.0	0.0	0.0	0.0	0.0	0.0	0.0	0.0	0.0	0.0	0.0	0.0
Max	5.0	5.0	5.0	5.0	5.0	5.0	5.0	5.0	5.0	5.0	5.0	5.0	5.0

Source: Data from Uganda 2012/13 UNHS survey.

ters (the qualitative work suggests than in some cases, distances are even longer). It takes about an hour on average for a household to get water—including both the time to go to the water source and the time spent waiting at the source. But for some households, the nearest water source is up to two hours away (this may be due to difficult terrain in some cases) and some households have to wait up to three hours when they arrive at the source to get water, although these are extremes. The poor tend to live farther away from water sources, and also tend to have to wait longer to get water, but the differences between quintiles are not very large, in part because access to piped water connection remains so limited. As expected, water sources are located closer to dwellings and take less time to visit in Kampala than in other cities, with longer distances in rural areas (estimates of the time required for households to obtain drinking from the 2011 Demographic and Health Survey are also provided in annex).

Finally, table 2.5 provides an assessment by community leaders from the community module of the 2012/13 survey of changes in the last two years in the access to safe water. On average, there is some improvement, since in a third of communities (33.3 percent) community leaders suggest an improvement, while there is deterioration in only in a fifth of the communities (20.9 percent). But things have remained unchanged in more than a third of the communities (36.3 percent). In one in ten communities (9.5 percent), there is simply no safe

Table 2.5 Community-Level Change in Availability of Safe Water and Efforts to Improve Water, 2012/13
Percent

	Location			Region				Welfare tercile			
	Kampala	Other urban	Rural	Central	Eastern	Northern	Western	1	2	3	Total
Change, past 2 years											
Improvement	16.3	32.6	34.8	37.2	17.7	39.8	40.3	33.9	27.8	36.5	33.3
No change	34.5	39.2	35.6	28.4	43.7	35.5	39.2	40.5	35.3	34.3	36.3
Deterioration	31.9	20.3	20.2	20.9	29.2	20.8	11.4	20.0	25.0	18.8	20.9
No safe water	17.4	8.0	9.4	13.5	9.4	3.9	9.2	5.7	11.9	10.5	9.5
Total	100.0	100.0	100.0	100.0	100.0	100.0	100.0	100.0	100.0	100.0	100.0
Projects undertaken											
Yes	12.5	31.8	32.0	50.5	29.4	16.3	18.6	20.9	34.8	34.7	30.9
No	87.5	68.2	68.0	49.5	70.6	83.7	81.4	79.1	65.2	65.3	69.1
Total	100.0	100.0	100.0	100.0	100.0	100.0	100.0	100.0	100.0	100.0	100.0
Types of projects											
Tree planting	17.7	23.1	26.3	10.4	29.2	72.6	37.2	48.0	23.3	17.8	25.3
Wetland encroachment	49.0	51.2	52.0	63.4	51.5	27.4	28.5	38.3	48.2	59.4	51.8
Forest encroachment	10.9	11.9	6.0	9.0	4.3	0.0	13.0	5.1	6.3	9.1	7.5
Other	22.4	13.8	15.7	17.2	15.1	0.0	21.3	8.5	22.2	13.7	15.4
Total	100.0	100.0	100.0	100.0	100.0	100.0	100.0	100.0	100.0	100.0	100.0

Source: Data from Uganda 2012/13 UNHS survey.

water, with differences in that proportion related more to location than welfare status (communities are ranked into three terciles according to the average level of consumption per equivalent adults of households living in the community, as measured through the household survey module).

When asked if communities have undertaken activities to protect water catchment areas, less than a third (30.9 percent) of community leaders respond in the affirmative. The proportion was lower in the poorest communities, with differences also observed between geographic areas. The most likely projects being undertaken are related to the prevention of wetland encroachment (51.8 percent of the communities), tree plantings (25.3 percent), other initiatives (15.4 percent), and finally the prevention of forest encroachment (7.5 percent).

Constraints for Access to Safe Water

The qualitative work in subsequent chapters provides a rich analysis of the constraints faced by households and communities to gain access to improved and safe water sources. But one question asked in a different survey—the 2010/11 Uganda National Panel Survey—already provides some insights. As shown in table 2.6, in Kampala, cost (the fact that the source of safe water requires a

Table 2.6 Reasons Declared by Households for Not Using Protected Water Sources, 2010/11

Percent

	Location			Region				Welfare quintile					Total
	Kampala	Other urban	Rural	Central	Eastern	Northern	Western	1	2	3	4	5	
Long distance	31.3	44.3	54.0	43.9	29.1	80.3	55.7	52.2	55.7	55.9	60.6	36.5	53.4
Unreliable	0.0	16.8	4.2	6.1	7.5	3.5	2.9	3.6	3.7	5.1	2.7	10.1	4.6
Water does not taste good	0.0	0.0	2.7	2.3	9.2	0.0	1.6	6.0	0.6	0.3	3.8	2.3	2.6
Require contribution	42.7	4.3	1.9	3.8	3.5	3.2	0.1	2.5	1.8	3.4	0.5	3.1	2.3
Long queues	0.0	0.0	0.0	0.1	0.0	0.0	0.0	0.0	0.0	0.0	0.3	0.0	0.0
Open source is okay	8.6	7.5	18.5	21.0	34.7	0.4	18.8	16.0	19.5	19.7	14.3	21.1	18.0
Other	17.4	27.1	18.8	22.7	16.0	12.6	20.9	19.8	18.7	15.6	17.9	26.9	19.1
Total	100.0	100.0	100.0	100.0	100.0	100.0	100.0	100.0	100.0	100.0	100.0	100.0	100.0

Source: Data from Uganda 2010/11 Panel survey.

financial contribution) seems to be a key factor, at least for those choosing to not use a safe water source. In other geographic areas, distance and perceptions that open water sources are good enough are mentioned much more. The fact that in Kampala the cost of safe water sources is considered high by some households could reflect a concern about the cost of a water network (in terms of connection costs especially as opposed to consumption tariffs), but it could also reflect a concern about the price of water at public taps or standpipes, which may be higher than it should be, as will be discussed in chapter 3. As to the fact that cost is not mentioned very much for other geographic areas in table 2.6, it does not imply—as the qualitative work will show, that affordability is not an issue. Often households do not have access to safe water sources, and the cost of boiling water (with charcoal or wood) may be too expensive for many, whether this is in term of out-of-pocket or opportunity (time use) cost.

Information from community leaders on the cost of water for households is also available in the community module of the 2012/13 survey, and this information suggests that cost is indeed a factor when households must pay for water (see table 2.7). In response to a question on whether people in the community pay for using water, community leaders respond in the affirmative in 36.9 percent of the communities. The average price is U Sh 178 per jerry can, with a median price of U Sh 100, although qualitative work in subsequent chapters suggests that in dry seasons prices are often higher. In areas with payments, the payments are typically required as user fees or tariffs (in 51.3 percent of communities) or for maintenance costs (in 45 percent of communities). The average monthly cost of water for households are estimated by community leaders at U Sh 12,451 (the median is U Sh 6,000), with large differences between areas probably resulting from both differences in water quality and levels of consumption. While the poor tend to have lower costs, this does not imply that as a share of their consumption (burden) the amounts that they must spend on water are lower and perceived by them as affordable. Finally, when asked whether the cost of water is affordable, community leaders suggest that this is the case in less than a third of the communities (30.2 percent). Somewhat surprisingly, the lowest shares of leaders considering water costs as affordable are observed in the richest communities and in Kampala, but this could possibly result from higher levels of consumption and unit costs there. In the qualitative work, it is clear that the poor in rural communities face more severe constraints, even when they do not have to pay for water, because they often cannot afford to make the water that they get safe.

One additional important indicator that is not available in the Uganda National Household Surveys, but is available in the 2011 Demographic and Health Survey, is whether households treat the water they drink before actually drinking it. The basic statistics are provided in annex. Less than half of the households use an appropriate treatment (mostly boiling the water, but in a few cases also adding water guard, bleach or chlorine, or straining the water

Table 2.7 Community Indicators on the Cost and Affordability of Water, 2012/13
Percent

	Location			Region				Welfare tercile			
	Kampala	Other urban	Rural	Central	Eastern	Northern	Western	1	2	3	Total
Payment for water (%)											
Yes	42.9	30.7	38.4	33.6	36.9	15.3	60.6	27.5	40.8	40.4	36.9
No	57.1	69.3	61.6	66.4	63.1	84.7	39.4	72.5	59.2	59.6	63.1
Total	100.0	100.0	100.0	100.0	100.0	100.0	100.0	100.0	100.0	100.0	100.0
Cost per jerry can (USh)											
Mean	151	293	138	94	186	84	233	50	90	236	178
Median	100	50	100	20	100	50	100	10	100	100	100
Types of payment (%)											
User fees/tariffs	71.0	63.6	46.5	61.2	8.0	15.3	82.4	21.5	49.8	65.7	51.3
Maintenance costs	17.0	34.8	50.1	34.6	87.7	74.8	16.3	77.0	45.3	30.5	45.0
Other	12.0	1.7	3.4	4.2	4.3	9.9	1.4	1.5	4.9	3.8	3.7
Total	100.0	100.0	100.0	100.0	100.0	100.0	100.0	100.0	100.0	100.0	100.0
Cost for households (USh)											
Mean (monthly)	34,897	16,513	9,489	17,703	1,845	3,223	18,342	5,475	9,521	17,741	12,451
Median (monthly)	30,000	15,000	2,000	10,000	500	1,000	18,000	1,000	3,000	15,000	6,000
Affordability of cost (%)											
Yes	20.7	24.8	32.3	29.7	41.1	35.1	21.6	37.4	32.6	25.3	30.2
No	79.3	75.2	67.7	70.3	58.9	65.0	78.5	62.6	67.4	74.7	69.8
Total	100.0	100.0	100.0	100.0	100.0	100.0	100.0	100.0	100.0	100.0	100.0

Source: Data from Uganda 2012/13 UNHS survey.

through cloth). As will be discussed in chapter 4 with the qualitative work, a number of constraints, including cost and lack of time, as well as perceptions that the water is safe enough, lead households not to use the appropriate treatments.

Still another way to look at the issue of the constraints faced by households and communities to gain access to improved and safe water sources consists in implementing a simple quantitative analysis of some of the feedback received from communities in the qualitative fieldwork. In chapter 4, the data from the qualitative fieldwork are organized along two thematic issues—first the issue of the availability of water, and then the issue of its quality and the measures that households could take, but are often not able to take, to improve quality. Before concluding this chapter, it is useful to briefly summarize quantitatively

Figure 2. 1 Challenges Associated with Accessing Safe and Clean Water

a. Urban

b. Rural

Source: Qualitative fieldwork in this study.

and in a visual way some of the issues mentioned by households in the qualitative fieldwork.

This is done in figure 2.1 on the basis of a classification of responses from focus-group participants to the following question: *"What are the challenges associated with accessing safe and clean water in this community?"* The idea in the rapid empirical results provided here is not to conduct any in-depth analysis of the responses to those questions provided in focus groups (this is done in chapter 4), but to note some of the broad themes considered by respondents.

As visualized in the figure, on the basis of a simple count of responses to that question agreed to by focus groups, concerns of adequacy, affordability, and costs, as well as waiting time and functionality of the water infrastructure (much of which does not function because of poor operation and maintenance procedures), dominate in urban areas. In rural areas, affordability is even more of an issue, which is not surprising, given that households are poorer there. In addition to adequacy and functionality which are also mentioned in rural areas, concerns are also raised about the quality of the available water, the distance to water sources, and even attitudes (for example, with respect to boiling water) and corruption in management.

Conclusion

The objective of this chapter was to provide a basic diagnostic of trends in access to alternative water sources in Uganda on the basis of nationally representative household surveys, and to discuss some of the constraints faced by households in accessing safe water, relying on both household surveys data and some of the data collected through focus groups in qualitative fieldwork. The data suggest that only a small minority of households have access to piped water, whether in the dwelling or through public standpipes. When considering other water sources considered as improved under the definitions adopted by the JMP for water and sanitation of the World Health Organization, the household surveys suggest that about three in four households can be considered as having access to improved water sources. This proportion is slightly higher in the last two rounds of the Uganda National Household Survey (for 2005/06 and 2012/13) than in the first two rounds (for 2002/03 and 2005/06).

A number of constraints to access to safe water can be identified in the surveys, as well as in qualitative fieldwork. Survey data suggest that cost is a factor for some households in not accessing safe water sources while they could in principle get access, especially in Kampala. In other areas, the distance to safe water sources and perceptions that open water sources are good enough are also at play. Community leaders tend to confirm that water may not always be affordable for some households when they have to pay for it, suggesting that these households have to sacrifice other basic necessities to purchase water. These cost and affordability constraints appear to be more prevalent concerns in the richest communities and in Kampala, where households are better off but where a larger share of the population indeed pays for water. By contrast, in some rural areas, water may not be safe, but it may be available for free from open water sources, although there could also be affordability constraints there in terms of the inability of communities to put in place systems that would make the water safer.

A rapid quantitative analysis of some of the responses provided by participants in focus groups on the challenge they face in accessing safe water suggests that concerns of adequacy, affordability, and costs, as well as waiting time and functionality of the water infrastructure, dominate in urban areas. In rural areas, affordability is even more of an issue (a finding that differs somewhat from the simple tabulations obtained from the household surveys), in conjunction with concerns about the adequacy, functionality, and quality of water sources, as well as the distance to the sources. Clearly, overall, many households face substantial challenges in accessing safe water. The more detailed qualitative analysis provided in chapter 4 provides a richer understanding of the challenges and constraints faced by households in accessing safe water—as well as some of their ongoing efforts to improve water sources in their communities.

Annex 2A: Access to Water Estimates from the 2011 DHS

Table 2A.1 Source of Household Drinking Water in the 2011 DHS
Percent

	Households			Population		
	Urban	*Rural*	*Total*	*Urban*	*Rural*	*Total*
Source of drinking water						
Improved source	90.6	65.6	70.3	89.6	66.6	70.0
Piped into dwelling/yard/plot	27.9	1.5	6.4	28.4	1.3	5.3
Public tap/standpipe	38.9	8.2	13.9	34.9	7.8	11.7
Borehole	11.8	43.9	37.9	16.1	45.9	41.6
Protected well/spring	6.9	10.2	9.6	7.6	10.2	9.8
Rainwater	0.5	1.4	1.3	0.4	1.3	1.2
Bottled water	4.6	0.4	1.2	2.1	0.1	0.4
Nonimproved source	8.9	33.6	29.0	10.1	32.8	29.5
Unprotected well/spring	5.6	18.2	15.8	7.0	17.6	16.1
Tanker truck/vendor	2.2	0.9	1.1	1.6	0.6	0.8
Surface water	1.0	14.6	12.0	1.4	14.5	12.6
Other source	0.6	0.8	0.7	0.3	0.6	0.5
Total	100.0	100.0	100.0	100.0	100.0	100.0
Percentage using improved water source	90.6	65.6	70.3	89.6	66.6	70.0
Time to obtain drinking water (round trip)						
Water on premises	40.1	6.2	12.5	37.4	5.4	10.0
Less than 30 minutes	42.8	31.1	33.3	41.5	29.7	31.4
30 minutes or longer	16.6	62.0	53.5	20.7	64.3	57.9
Don't know/missing	0.5	0.7	0.7	0.4	0.6	0.6
Total	100.0	100.0	100.0	100.0	100.0	100.0
Water treatment before drinking						
Boiled	70.6	37.7	43.9	68.8	34.8	39.8
Added water guard	3.3	2.7	2.8	3.6	2.6	2.8
Bleach/chlorine added	0.1	0.2	0.2	0.1	0.2	0.2
Strained through cloth	0.8	1.4	1.3	1.0	1.6	1.5
Ceramic, sand, or other filter	0.5	0.5	0.5	0.5	0.5	0.5
Solar disinfection	0.0	0.2	0.2	0.1	0.2	0.1
Let it stand and settle	0.3	0.6	0.5	0.4	0.5	0.5
Other	0.5	0.4	0.4	0.5	0.4	0.4
No treatment	26.7	58.9	52.8	27.8	61.6	56.6
Percentage using appropriate treatment	72.8	40.8	46.8	71.6	38.0	43.0
Number	1,691	7,342	9,033	6,468	37,782	44,250

Source: 2011 UDHS survey report.

Note

1. That survey is not used in the study because the questions asked about access to water are not sufficiently disaggregated for the type of analysis carried in the study.

References

Alderman, H., L. Elder, A. Goyal, A. Herforth, Y. T. Hoberg, A., Marini, J. Ruel-Bergeron, J. Saavedra, M. Shekar, and S. Tiwari. 2013. *Improving Nutrition through Multisectoral Approaches*. Washington, DC: World Bank.

Barungi, M., and I. Kasirye. 2011. *Cost-effectiveness of Water Interventions: The Case for Public-stand Pipes and Bore-holes in Reducing Diarrhea among Urban Children in Uganda*. Kampala, Uganda: Economic Policy Research Center.

Bbaale, E., and F. Buyinza. 2012. "Micro-analysis of Mother's Education and Child Mortality: Evidence from Uganda." *Journal of International Development* 24 (S1): S138–58.

Bhutta, Z., T. Ahmet, R. Black, S. Cousens, K. Dewey, E. Giugliani, B. Haider, B. Kirkwood, S. Morris, H. Sachdev, M. Shekar, and the Maternal and Child Undernutrition Study Group. 2008. "What Works? Interventions for Maternal and Child Undernutrition and Survival." *The Lancet* 371 (9610): 417–40.

Blackden, M., and Q. Wodon, eds. 2006. *Gender, Time Use, and Poverty*. Washington, DC: World Bank.

Cairncross, S., C. Hunt, S. Boisson, K. Bostoen, V. Curtis, I. Fung, and W. Schmidt. 2010. "Water, Sanitation and Hygiene for the Prevention of Diarrhea." *International Journal of Epidemiology* 39 (Suppl. 1): i193–205.

Denboba, A., R. Sayre, Q. Wodon, L. Elder, L. Rawlings, and J. Lombardi. 2014. *Stepping up Early Childhood Development: Investing in Young Children with High Returns*. Washington, DC: World Bank.

Diallo, A., and Q. Wodon. 2007. "Demographic Transition towards Smaller Household Sizes and Basic Infrastructure Needs in Developing Countries." *Economics Bulletin* 15 (11): 1–11.

Dillingham, R., and R. L. Guerrant. 2004. "Childhood Stunting: Measuring and Stemming the Staggering Costs of Inadequate Water and Sanitation." *The Lancet* 363 (9403): 94–5.

Esrey, A. 1996. "Water, Waste, and Well-being: A Multi-Country Study." *American Journal of Epidimiology* 143 (6): 608.

Esrey, S. A., J. B. Potash, L. Roberts, and C. Shiff. 1991. "Effects of Improved Water Supply and Sanitation on Ascariasis, Diarrhoea, Dracunculiasis, Hookworm Infection, Schistosomiasis, and Trachoma." *Bulletin of the World Health Organization* 69 (5): 609–21.

Fay, M., D. Leipziger, Q. Wodon, and T. Yepes. 2005. "Achieving Child-Health-Related Millennium Development Goals: The Role of Infrastructure." *World Development* 33 (8): 1267–84.

Hutton, G., and L. Haller. 2004. *Evaluation of the Costs and Benefits of Water and Sanitation Improvements at the Global Level*. Geneva: World Health Organization.

Jalan, J., and M. Ravallion. 2003. "Does Piped Water Reduce Diarrhea for Children in Rural India?" *Journal of Econometrics* 112: 153–73.

Kosek, M., C. Bern, and L. R. Guerrant. 2003. "The Global Burden of Diarrheal Disease, as Estimated from Studies Published between 1992 and 2000." *Bulletin of the World Health Organization* 81: 197–204.

Moe, L. C., and D. R. Rheingans. 2006. "Global Challenges in Water, Sanitation and Health." *Journal of Water and Health* 04 (Suppl.): 41–57.

Rijsberman, F., and A. P. Zwane. 2012. "Copenhagen Consensus 2012 Challenge Paper: Water and Sanitation." http://www.copenhagenconsensus.com.

Schuster-Wallace, J. C., I. V. Grover, Z. Adeel, U. Confalonieri, and S. Elliot. 2008. *Safe Water as the Key to Global Health.* Hamilton, Ontario, Canada: United Nations University International Network on Water.

Spears, D. 2013. "How Much International Variation in Child Height Can Sanitation Explain?" Policy Research Working Paper No. 6351, World Bank, Washington, DC.

Tsimpo, C., and Q. Wodon. 2017. *Residential Piped Water in Uganda.* Washington, DC: World Bank.

World Bank. 2010. *Water and Development: An Evaluation of World Bank Support, 1997–2007.* Washington, DC: World Bank.

———. 2015. "Review of Uganda's 2006 Pro-Poor Strategy for Water And Sanitation." World Bank, Washington, DC.

Zwane, A. P., and M. Kremer. 2007. "What Works in Fighting Diarrheal Diseases in Developing Countries? A Critical Review." *World Bank Research Observer* 22 (1): 1–24.

CHAPTER 3

Cost of Public Taps and Alternative Water Sources

Clarence Tsimpo and Quentin Wodon

Introduction

The data provided in chapter 2 suggests that in Kampala especially but also in other areas, the cost of water may be an issue for some, and potentially many households. When households are not connected to the water network and are forced to rely on other water providers, as may be the case in urban areas, they may end up paying a higher price per unit of consumption than households that benefit from a connection to the network. This could be the case not only for tankers and street vendors but also for public taps (or standpipes) because of the role played by intermediaries in operating the taps. Even though the water at public taps may be provided at a lower price by utilities than that charged to residential customers connected to the network, the price for end users may be higher because of the operating costs and profits reaped by (often private) tap operators. This chapter first summarizes briefly the data on the sources of water used by households, noting that most households and especially the poor do not have domestic water connections. The chapter then measures the cost of water from public taps and compares it with the cost of other sources of water. The results indicate that despite the reduced price per cubic meter charged by utilities, the prices for end users are higher at the taps than the prices paid by residential customers directly connected to the network.

Basic infrastructure services help in meeting basic needs and improving human development indicators related to education and health. However, infrastructure services may be costly, and many households in Sub-Saharan Africa either cannot afford the services or live too far away from existing networks to connect. In the case of water, public utilities typically provide not only domestic connections (with the cost of consumption often subsidized; see Angel-Urdinola and Wodon 2007, as well as Komives et al. 2005, 2007; Banerjee et al. 2008, 2010; Estache and Wodon 2014) but also public taps that serve large numbers of households.

In principle, water at public taps should be affordable, because utilities sell the water to the operator at a subsidized cost. This is the case in Uganda, where the largest provider of piped water—the National Water and Sewerage Corporation (NWSC 2013)—charges a lower unit price per cubic meter to the operators of public standpipes or taps than is the case for residential and other classes of customers (especially when sewerage charges are accounted for).

As shown in table 3.1, the price for water at public taps in Uganda is at only at about two-thirds of the price paid by residential customers. However, if households benefit from sewerage service, an additional charge is levied at 75 percent of the water tariff for domestic customers and 100 percent for other categories of customers. Sewerage charges are based on the volume of water consumed. An overall price per cubic meter including sewerage charges has thereby also been included in the table, and the prices have been provided as well by jerry can of 20 liter.

The question considered in this chapter is whether households relying on public taps pay a lower price for the water they consume than households connected to the network. The answer to that question is not clear à priori, because in many countries residential customers are also subsidized. In addition, operators of public taps charge fees for their services, and this may lead to higher costs for households. Finally, some of the water made available through public taps may be resold by street vendors at an even higher price, given that the water is then typically brought to the household dwelling. Paradoxically then, we may well have situations whereby better-off households that are connected to the network pay less per unit of consumption than poorer households without access, which, in the case of water, need to rely on public taps or vendors. The contribution of this chapter is to estimate the unit costs of service provision for water not only by service provider but also by household welfare status in Uganda.

The paper broadly follows the approach outlined in Bardasi and Wodon (2008). Using data from Niger, these authors found that in the capital city of Niamey,

Table 3.1 NWSC Tariff Structure for Fiscal Year 2012/13

Customer category	Cubic meter	Jerry can	Sewerage per m³ [a]	Total per m³	Total per jerry can
Public standpipe	1,236	24.72	0	1,236	24.72
Domestic (residential)	1,912	38.24	1,434	3,346	66.92
Institutions and government	2,353	47.06	2,353	4,706	94.12
Commercial up to 500 m³	2,887	57.74	2,887	5,774	115.48
Commercial between 500 m³ and 1,500 m³	2,887	57.74	2,887	5,774	115.48
Commercial above 1,500 m³	2,462	49.24	2,462	4,924	98.48
Weighted water tariff	2,290	n.a.	n.a.	n.a.	n.a.

Source: NWRC.
Note: n.a. = not applicable. a. Value-added tax not included. A jerry can has a capacity of 20 liters. Only when there are sewerage services. The sewer tariff is 75 percent of the water tariff for domestic customers and 100 percent for other categories of customers. Sewerage charge is based on volume of water consumed. NWRC = National Water and Sewerage Corporation.

despite the fact that the water sold at public fountains benefited from a social tariff for the (private) tap operator, the average price paid by households at the taps was three times higher than the average price paid for piped water by households with a private connection to the network. Even more expensive was a cubic meter of water bought from street vendors (*porteurs d'eau*), at an average of five times the residential price of the network. In this chapter, we use data from Uganda's national surveys to carry similar estimations. While the results are not as extreme as in Niger, it does appear that users of public taps pay as much for their water as domectic customers despite the price reduction granted to public tap operators by NWSC. Section 2 provides data on the shares of households using alternative sources of drinking water. Section 3 documents the unit cost of these sources of water for households among those paying for water. A conclusion follows.

Sources of Drinking Water

As mentioned in chapter 2, data are available in various surveys on the sources of drinking water for households. In chapter 2, the analysis relied on both the cross-sectional national Uganda household surveys for statistics on sources of drinking water and the Uganda national panel survey (qualitative fieldwork was also used). The panel survey has a smaller sample size, but the questions asked about cost in that survey are more detailed than in the larger cross-sectional national survey. The panel survey also has an interesting question on the reasons for not using safe water sources. It was shown that in Kampala cost (the fact that safe water sources require a financial contribution) is a key factor for not using safe water when it is in principle available. Distance to safe water sources was also mentioned as an issue, although less so in Kampala than in other areas. Finally, feelings that open water sources are good enough were mentioned quite often as reasons not to rely on safe water sources in rural areas.

The fact that in Kampala the cost of safe water sources is considered high by some households could reflect a concern about the cost of piped water obtained through domestic connections to the network (probably more in terms of connection than consumption costs once connected), but it could also reflect a concern about the price of water at public taps/standpipes for those not having a private connection, and this is a rather large group of households.

How large is the household group relying on public standpipes? Summary statistics from the national cross-sectional survey on alternative sources of drinking water are provided in table 3.2 for the last two survey years (2009/10 and 2012/13). These are reproduced (in shorter form with fewer categories in columns) from chapter 2 for readers who may have skipped that chapter. The response modalities differ slightly between the two surveys, but public taps (or standpipes) play an important role, serving a larger share of households than private connections. Note that in terms of the population served, there has been an expansion of private connections between the two surveys, while the share of households relying on public taps has decreased over time.

Table 3.2 Main Source of Drinking Water, 2009/10 and 2012/13

	Residence area		Welfare quintile					
	Rural	Urban	Q1	Q2	Q3	Q4	Q5	Total
				2009/10				
Private connection to pipeline	1.7	19.8	1.2	0.7	1.3	1.9	15.1	5.1
Public taps	5.1	47.2	3.1	6.0	6.8	14.7	25.9	13.0
Borehole	39.7	11.6	47.8	40.4	38.8	34.5	20.1	34.4
Protected well/spring	20.5	12.8	18.0	22.5	23.2	21.3	13.1	19.1
River, stream, lake, pond	26.6	2.4	26.9	27.9	24.4	21.7	14.5	22.1
Vendor/tanker truck	2.1	4.0	0.0	0.7	1.0	2.3	6.0	2.5
Gravity flow scheme	1.3	0.5	1.2	0.9	1.8	1.2	0.9	1.2
Rainwater	1.1	0.4	0.2	0.4	0.6	1.0	2.0	1.0
Other	1.7	1.4	1.6	0.6	2.0	1.4	2.4	1.7
Total	100.0	100.0	100.0	100.0	100.0	100.0	100.0	100.0
				2012/13				
Piped water in dwelling	0.3	5.6	0.0	0.0	0.5	0.8	5.2	1.7
Piped water in the yard	1.0	17.3	0.0	0.8	2.3	5.2	13.3	5.3
Public taps	5.3	24.9	2.9	5.0	8.0	11.7	19.2	10.6
Borehole in yard/plot	0.6	1.0	0.7	0.6	0.7	0.6	0.9	0.7
Public borehole	39.4	21.4	50.0	43.8	38.8	30.1	20.8	34.6
Protected well/spring	17.8	14.2	13.7	22.4	17.1	18.2	14.0	16.8
Unprotected well/spring	22.3	6.8	18.7	17.1	22.1	21.6	13.4	18.2
River/stream/lake	8.2	1.7	9.7	6.1	7.0	7.0	4.1	6.5
Vendor	1.1	3.8	0.2	0.4	1.1	1.7	4.2	1.8
Tanker truck	0.1	0.0	0.0	0.1	0.0	0.0	0.1	0.1
Gravity flow scheme	1.9	0.7	3.6	2.4	1.3	1.3	0.5	1.6
Rainwater	1.3	1.0	0.2	0.7	0.7	1.2	2.5	1.2
Bottled water	0.2	1.0	0.0	0.0	0.0	0.0	1.4	0.4
Other	0.6	0.4	0.5	0.7	0.6	0.5	0.5	0.5
Total	100.0	100.0	100.0	100.0	100.0	100.0	100.0	100.0

Source: Data from Uganda 2009/10 and 2012/13 UNHS surveys.

Other sources of drinking water include boreholes in yards/plots, public boreholes, protected wells/springs, unprotected wells/springs, rivers/streams/lakes, water vendors, tanker trucks, gravity flow schemes, rainwater, bottled water, and other water sources. The three main sources overall for the population as a whole, a large majority of which lives in rural areas, are public boreholes, protected wells/springs, unprotected wells/springs. These are sources of water on which the poor rely heavily, as shown by the concentration curves in figures 3.1 and 3.2, but it is worth pointing out that households relying on public stand pipes are as expected better off than the overall population, but less well off than those with private connections.

Figure 3.1 Concentration Curves for Sources of Drinking Water, 2009/10

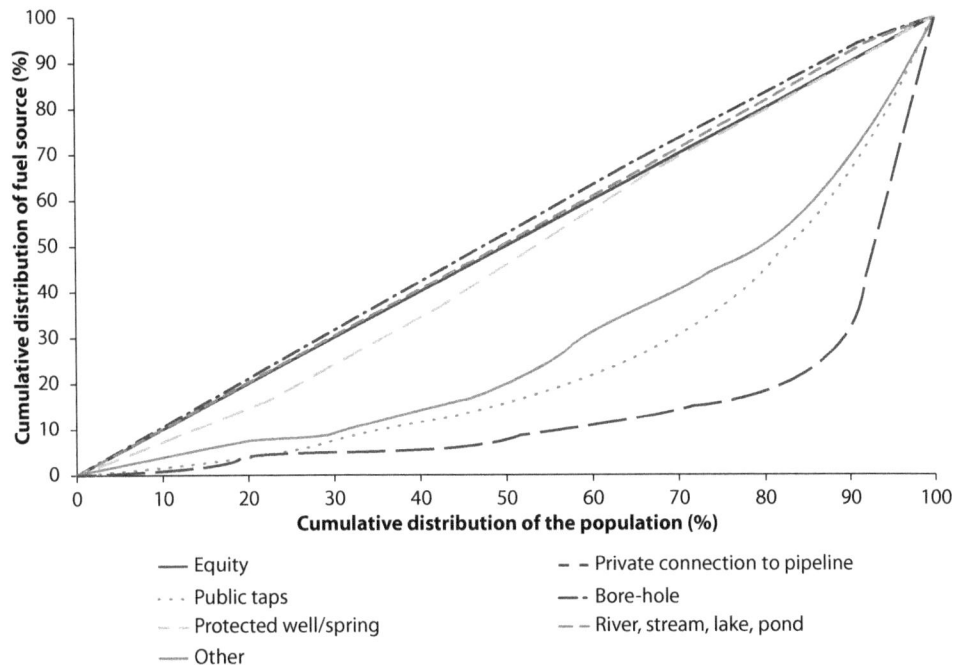

Legend:
— Equity
··· Public taps
– – Protected well/spring
— Other
– – Private connection to pipeline
—·– Bore-hole
– – River, stream, lake, pond

Source: Data from Uganda 2009/10 UNHS surveys.

Figure 3.2 Concentration Curves for Sources of Drinking Water, 2012/13

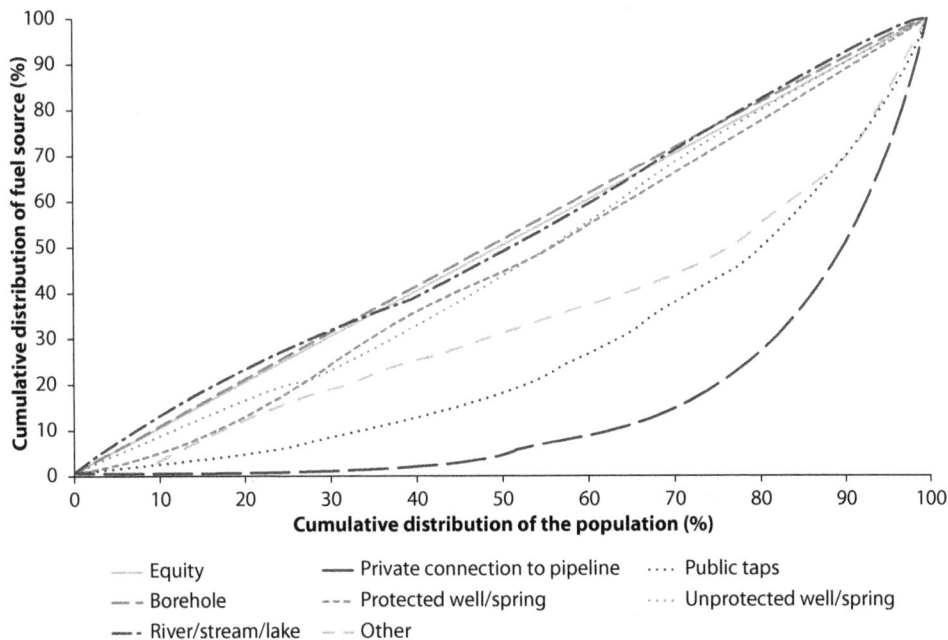

Legend:
— Equity
–·– Borehole
—·– River/stream/lake
— Private connection to pipeline
– – – Protected well/spring
– – Other
···· Public taps
···· Unprotected well/spring

Source: Data from Uganda 2012/13 UNHS surveys.

Cost of Alternative Sources of Water

For the purpose of this chapter, the comparison of interest is in terms of the cost of water for different types of water sources, and for this the most appropriate data source is the 2010/11 Uganda national panel survey. In that survey, detailed information is provided by households on the price of the water that they rely on. A large majority of households (95.4 percent) reported the price of water per jerry can of 20 liter and another 4.7 percent per liter. Only 0.23 percent used other units, and these households are not included in the analysis because of the difficulty of translating those units in liters of jerry cans. Table 3.3 provides information on the share of households paying for water and the average and median prices paid for water (among those paying for water, thus excluding zero values) for the main sources of water requiring payment.

About a third of the population is paying for water, but the proportion is much higher in Kampala where more than three fourths of households pay for their water, and in other cities where the proportion is two thirds. Yet even in rural areas about a fourth of households pay for water. There are also large differences between regions, and especially by quintiles of welfare.

In terms of the median and average prices paid, the most expensive water source is (not surprisingly) a vendor or tanker truck for which the median and average prices are respectively 200 U Sh and 219.4 U Sh per jerry can (the two categories have been aggregated because of relatively limited sample sizes). Next are private connections to the network, with median and average prices of 111.1 U Sh and 127.3 U Sh per jerry can, respectively. These prices are substantially higher than the unit price charged by NWSC indicated in table 3.1, which was U Sh 66.92 per jerry can including the sewerage charge. Only a small part of the difference can be attributed to the additional fixed charge of U Sh 1,500 that households must pay every month when connected to the network. This suggests that connected households may be overestimating the unit cost of their water consumption. This risk of overestimation should be less likely for households using public taps or vendors, since when you have to purchase water daily, you typically do know the price you have to pay. Thus, while on face value the price paid by connected households is slightly higher than the price paid by house-holds using public taps, the reverse may be true in practice, which would add to the concern about the relatively high price of water at public taps.

The unit price for those purchasing their water from public taps, at 100 U Sh per jerry can for the median and 106.1 U Sh per jerry can for the mean, is much higher than the discounted price charged by NWSC to the public tap operators, at U Sh 24.72 per jerry can (without VAT). This would suggest that public taps operators may be charging quite a bit to households for their intermediation function, thereby not making public tap water as affordable for households at it should be. Said differently, the median and average unit prices for public tap water are fairly close to those declared by households connected to the network (and possibly above those prices if connected households overestimate the price they pay), and are much higher than actual network prices including sewerage

Table 3.3 Cost of Water for Households Paying for Water, 2010/11

	Location			Region				Welfare quintile					Total
	Kampala	Other town	Rural	Central	Eastern	Northern	Western	Q1	Q2	Q3	Q4	Q5	
Share paying for water													
Yes	76.4	66.7	24.9	48.3	29.9	39.4	10.8	15.3	22.8	26.2	37.7	60.1	32.3
No	23.6	33.3	75.1	51.7	70.1	60.6	89.2	84.7	77.2	73.9	62.3	40.0	67.7
Total	100.0	100.0	100.0	100.0	100.0	100.0	100.0	100.0	100.0	100.0	100.0	100.0	100.0
Average price, 20 liters													
Private connection	153.6	112.7	122.7	144.3	75.8	121.1	100.3	–	72.2	75.5	112.5	135.5	127.3
Public taps	106.2	107.3	104.7	118.5	78.2	76.4	90.2	55.0	82.4	90.0	99.5	117.1	106.1
Borehole	100.0	36.0	14.9	32.6	11.3	16.7	16.5	7.7	9.9	8.9	23.5	41.2	17.1
Protected well/spring	72.9	75.0	55.7	110.7	21.5	13.1	202.3	2.4	6.8	84.0	56.8	80.9	60.4
Vendor/tanker truck	139.5	152.4	231.8	241.2	333.3	–	115.4	–	–	200.0	237.2	209.2	219.4
Median price, 20 liters													
Private connection to pipeline	133.3	111.1	133.3	150.0	80.0	133.3	72.2	–	72.2	77.8	100.0	125.0	111.1
Public taps	100.0	100.0	100.0	100.0	100.0	100.0	100.0	100.0	93.3	100.0	100.0	100.0	100.0
Borehole	100.0	16.7	5.6	8.3	5.6	6.7	5.6	5.6	6.7	5.6	8.3	5.6	6.7
Protected well/spring	93.3	93.3	8.3	93.3	33.3	5.6	125.0	2.4	5.6	8.3	13.3	46.7	11.1
Vendor/tanker truck	100.0	166.7	300.0	300.0	333.3	–	100.0	–	–	200.0	300.0	166.7	200.0

Source: Data from 2010/11 panel survey.

charge, while in fact they should be below those levels. Although more detailed data would be needed for a more in-depth diagnostic, this could suggest that (some) public tap operators might overcharge households that rely on their service. What is clear in any case is that while the cost of water from public taps is meant to be substantially lower than that of water from domestic connections (especially when sewerage charges are included), it does not seem to be the case in practice. While the issue is not as severe as that documented by Bardasi and Wodon (2008) for the case of Niamey, it is a source of concern.

Conclusions

Access to piped water in Uganda is uneven across geographic areas and quintiles of wealth, with the better off being much more likely to be connected to the water network than the poor. In addition, households that are connected to the network may actually pay a lower price per cubic meter of water or jerry can than households relying on public taps, or at least the differences in prices are not as large as they should be. This may suggest that the costs and/or profits of tap operator may be high, thereby making public tap water less affordable than it should be. More in-depth analysis would be required to establish such suggestions, but the results of the analysis carried in this chapter point to a source of concern.

As noted in Bardasi and Wodon (2008), at least two types of policy interventions could help to remedy this situation. First, in the medium term, an expansion of the water network would lead to help to have more households benefiting from a connection. Second, better management and/or regulatory oversight for public tap operators could perhaps help in reducing the prices that users must pay to get their water there, while also probably leading to lower prices from street vendors who also often purchase their water from public taps. Despite the fact that the water sold to public taps is subsidized by the water utility, the prices requested by the private operators of these taps tend to be high and possibly higher than they should or possibly could be.

References

Angel-Urdinola, D., and Q. Wodon. 2007. "Do Utility Subsidies Reach the Poor? Framework and Evidence for Cape Verde, Sao Tome, and Rwanda." *Economics Bulletin* 9 (4): 1–7.

Banerjee, S., Q. Wodon, A. Diallo, T. Pushak, H. Uddin, C. Tsimpo, and V. Foster. 2008. "Access, Affordability and Alternatives: Modern Infrastructure Services in Africa." Africa Infrastructure Country Diagnostic Study Background Paper 2, World Bank, Washington, DC.

Banerjee, S., Q. Wodon, and V. Foster. 2010. "Dealing with Poverty and Inequality." In *Africa's Infrastructure: A Time for Transformation*, edited by V. Foster and C. Briceno-Garmendia. Washington, DC: Africa Development Forum, Agence Française de Développement and World Bank.

Bardasi, E., and Q. Wodon. 2008. "Who Pays the Most for Water? Alternative Providers and Service Costs in Niger." *Economics Bulletin* 9 (20): 1–10.

Estache, A., and Q. Wodon. 2014. *Infrastructure and Poverty in Sub-Saharan Africa.* New York: Palgrave Macmillan.

Komives, K., V. Foster, J. Halpern, and Q. Wodon, with support from R. Abdullah. 2005. *Water, Electricity, and the Poor: Who Benefits from Utility Subsidies?* Directions in Development. Washington, DC: World Bank.

Komives, K., J. Halpern, V. Foster, Q. Wodon, and R. Abdullah. 2007. "Residential Utility Subsidies as Targeted Transfer Mechanisms." *Development Policy Review* 25 (6): 659–79.

National Water and Sewerage Corporation. 2013. "Annual Activity Report for the FY 2012/13: Performance Review for the Period July 2012–June 2013." NWSC, Kampala.

CHAPTER 4

Challenges for Access to Safe Water: Qualitative Analysis

Clarence Tsimpo, Willy Kagarura, Nakafu Rose Kazibwe, John Ssenkumba Nsimbe, and Quentin Wodon

Introduction

This chapter complements the quantitative analysis of chapters 2 and 3 with a detailed qualitative analysis of some of the challenges and constraints faced by households in accessing safe water—as well their ongoing efforts to improve water sources in their communities. After a brief description of the methodology adopted for the qualitative fieldwork, the discussion of the data collected through focus groups and key informant interviews is organized along two thematic issues: the availability of water (with questions related to functionality, responsibility, and scarcity) and the quality of the water that is available, as well as the measures that households and communities could take, but may often not be able to take, to improve both availability and quality.

As noted in chapter 2, improved water sources are essential for good health and can have a major impact on child morbidity, malnutrition, and mortality (there is a very large literature on the links between water and sanitation on the one hand and health on the other; see among many others Esrey et al. 1991; Esrey, 1996; Kosek, Bern, and Guerrant 2003; Jalan and Ravallion, 2003; Dillingham and Guerrant 2004; Fay et al. 2005; Hutton and Haller 2004; Moe and Rheingans 2006; Zwane and Kremer 2007; Bhutta, Ahmet, and Black 2008; Schuster-Wallace et al. 2008; Cairncross, Hunt, and Boisson 2010; World Bank 2010; Rijsberman and Zwane 2012; Alderman et al. 2013; Spears 2013; Denboba et al. 2014). Access to safe water also improves the productivity of workers, not only through better health but also through time savings when safe water is available close enough to where households live (on access to water and time use, as well as time poverty, see Blackden and Wodon 2006). In Uganda, Bbaale, and Buyinza (2012) suggest that fetching water contributes to primary school absenteeism, while Tsimpo and Wodon (2014) show that access to piped water enables households to shift time from domestic to market work, thereby reducing poverty.

Chapters 2 and 3 provided a quantitative diagnostic of the access to improved water sources in Uganda and of the cost of some of those sources for households using nationally representative household surveys. Statistics were provided on trends in access to water according to the detailed modalities available in survey questionnaires and more aggregated definitions adopted by the Joint Monitoring Programme (JMP) for water and sanitation of the World Health Organization (WHO). Constraints to access to safe water were then discussed relying on both the household and community modules of existing surveys, including in chapter 3 for the assessment of the cost of alternative water sources for households. Finally, qualitative data on constraints faced by households were briefly analyzed quantitatively to provide a better understanding of some of the factors that limit access to safe water.

The focus in this chapter shifts to qualitative analysis. Before presenting the approach used for qualitative data collection, it may be worth mentioning some of the benefits that can be gained from qualitative data and from the combination of both approaches as the combination of quantitative and qualitative data is important and warranted by the nature of some of the questions being analyzed.[1] Quantitative data and methods have long been privileged in the development literature, especially in economics. They provide robustness to the results if they rely on appropriate samples, and regression analysis helps to control for a large number of other variables when measuring the impact of a specific variable on a given outcome. Yet, quantitative data often cannot capture well causal mechanisms, especially when the analysis fails to provide contextual information. Qualitative methods through focus groups and key informant interviews help to shed light on the economic, sociocultural, and political context of processes under study.

While quantitative analysis in development work is often goods- and services centered, qualitative research is often people centered (following Sen's work on the importance of freedom and capabilities to achieve functionings) and institutions centered (since the access to and use of services is driven by processes rather than a condition at a given point of time, the role of institutions in permitting or preventing access must be analyzed). Qualitative research also often contains both objective and subjective dimensions, to the degree that it considers both the objective conditions of people's lives and access to services and their perceptions about those services including feelings about their situation (this can also be done with quantitative data).

An important aspect of qualitative research methods refers to what scholars call research access. While no hasty conclusions should be made about the advantages of qualitative research techniques (respondents may refuse to be interviewed while they may accept to fill in an anonymous questionnaire), such methods are often better suited to address sensitive issues. In some cases, developing a relationship of trust with the "researched" is needed for data collection.

The need to adapt the language according to the type of actors under study is also important for the discovery of knowledge. In addition, accessing certain types of interviewees such as officials may be hard by simply sending out a questionnaire.

Another argument in favor of integrated research methods relates to the potential of complementing quantitative data with actor-oriented perspectives in applied research. An actor-oriented perspective entails the variety of social practices and at times incompatible worldviews between actors and the multiple realities to which these practices and worldviews respond. In the case of research on service delivery, key actors would include not only the various clients of the organizations providing the services but also the professionals providing those services, whether they work in private or public institutions. The experience and voice of clients, as well as the perspective of government professionals and private facilities' staffs at the different echelons of the service delivery process are often overlooked when relying only on quantitative survey data, or at least not systematically and rigorously researched.

Still another argument in favor of integrated research methods relates to policy making. Qualitative data derived from interviews and focus groups are often criticized for its subjectivity. This is a legitimate concern, and it underscores the fact that qualitative research methods must be implemented rigorously by well-trained researchers, with their results ideally supported by further quantitative analysis. But policy-oriented social analysis is concerned with change and agency—that is, how the beneficiaries of education services, the staffs in the field manning the facilities, and the policy makers can act outside and sometimes against a system which may reduce access to the services for the poor. In such contexts, the subjectivity of the various actors, and how as persons they perceive their situations of deprivation and/or lack of access to existing services, is crucial to understanding the basis of agency.

A potential problem with formal, objective, and often quantitative methods is that they may take for granted the context and relationships that constitutes the phenomena under study. At the other extreme, a subjective point of view may assert that social reality is an ongoing process that social actors continually reconstruct, failing to see the existing regularities. A key challenge for policy analysis is to analyze the objective conditions of reality while identifying how perceptions influence reality. Especially when it takes into consideration the rules, values, and perceptions of the individuals or groups involved, qualitative research may help to ensure that policies and programs are responsive to the needs of intended beneficiaries in all their social and cultural diversity. And while qualitative methods can help to enrich areas which have traditionally been dominated by quantitative research, the reverse is also true: quantitative methods can enrich these areas which have been dominated by qualitative research. Indeed, the absence or difficulty of quantification has been a factor in the still relatively slow systematic take up of research aiming to measure the contribution of faith-inspired providers of education services in Sub-Saharan Africa. In a nutshell, by combining quantitative and qualitative research methods, it is hoped that this study provides a more in-depth diagnostic of the issues considered.

In the case of the analysis of water and sanitation presented in this study, the qualitative data collection aimed to answer a number of questions that emerged from a review of the existing literature and the quantitative (household survey based) analysis of the water and sanitation sector. Some of the questions of interest were as follows: (1) What are the existing perceptions of what constitutes safe and clean water and what practices to improve water quality are undertaken at household level in various regions of Uganda; (2) what are the factors which determine access to safe water for different socioeconomic groups during different seasons of the year and what strategies are adopted to improve access for households?; (3) how has the availability of water for crop and animal husbandry affected people's socioeconomic livelihoods in different parts of Uganda?; (4) what trade-offs are considered in investing in hygienic toilet facilities at the household level and how can we explain the current low percentage of Ugandans who wash their hands with soap after visiting the toilet?; (5) what is the state of the public toilet system in schools, markets, health centers, and places of worship and what factors explain why they are in such a state?; and (6) what are the contrasting practices of waste water disposal in urban and rural areas and what are the implications and consequences of these practices?

The qualitative fieldwork was undertaken in 14 districts selected in such a way that at least one district was sampled from each geographical subregion of Uganda. In each region, districts were randomly selected from areas with varied water and sanitation performance grading in order to include good, fair, and poor-performing areas in terms of access to safe water in the sample. In addition, purposive targeting was used to select and include districts reflecting some of the main livelihood clusters (pastoralists, crop farmers, fishing) for households. Finally, in each district two communities, one urban and one rural, were visited. The selected districts (as well as their region) for the qualitative fieldwork are shown in table 4.1.

Table 4.1 Location of Sampled Districts for Qualitative Research on Water and Sanitation

Region	Districts	Number of districts
Central 1	Sembabule, Kiboga	2
Central 2	Kalangala	1
East Central	Bugiri	1
Eastern	Bukedea	1
Kampala Divisions	Kawempe	1
North/Mid-North	Lamwo, Apac	2
Karamoja/North East	Kotido, Amudat	2
West Nile	Moyo	1
Western/Mid-Western	Masindi	1
South Western	Kisoro, Bundibugyo	2
Total		14

Source: Qualitative fieldwork in this study.

The instruments used for the fieldwork included focus-group discussions (FGDs), key informant interviews, observations, and case studies. Before fieldwork activities, detailed checklists for FGDs and case studies were developed to guide the different categories of targeted populations. The categories of stakeholders that were targeted for data collection included community members (women, men, youth, elderly), leaders of water user committees, local government officials (CAOs, district water officers, district health inspectors, district health educators), and, at the national level, officials of National Water and Sewerage Corporation (NWSC), Ministry of Water and Environment, Ministry of Health officials, and Kampala Divisions Health Inspectors. Some visits to health centers and schools were also conducted to provide a physical assessment of the toilet facilities and provisions for hand washing, with observations and photographs made on site. Visits were also done to water projects like dams and pumping sites.

In what follows, the qualitative data obtained from the fieldwork are organized along two thematic issues—first the issue of the availability of water with questions related to functionality, responsibility, and scarcity (in section 2), and then the issue of the quality of the available water and the measures that households and communities could take, but may often not be able to take, to improve quality (in section 3). A brief conclusion follows.

Water Provision

In all 14 districts (28 communities, since one urban and one rural location were visited in each district), access to adequate water was found to be challenging. Water sources are limited in comparison to the number of people living in particular areas. Many communities have only a few water sources, and, in some cases, water is so scarce that households must rely on water harvesting during the rainy season to meet their needs. In some communities, households must travel long distance to get safe water or use water from unsafe sources such as swamps, ponds, and lakes. In other communities, water points were not functional at the time of the visits. Overall, lack of access to safe water, while resulting from multiple factors, can be broadly categorized as resulting in communities from lack of functionality because of poor maintenance, lack of local responsibility, and actual scarcity of water. The three issues are documented below.

Functionality

The Ministry of Water and Environment publishes an annual sector performance review. These reports suggest typically that about a fifth of water points are not functioning. Major causes for nonfunctionality include technical breakdowns and low yield. Shallow wells tend to have the lowest functionality rates, while protected springs have the highest functionality rate. Some water sources are considered as abandoned, having been nonfunctional for five or more years. Only about half of Water Source Committees are functioning properly. While levels of functionality have increased in urban areas, gains in rural areas have been weaker.

Lack of functionality is due to many factors, including dry/low yielding, low water quality, facilities that do not meet standards, and aging systems. But operations and maintenance is key. Construction of water and sanitation infrastructures can enhance people's health and well-being. But problems with operation and maintenance of equipment can reverse these gains. Operation and maintenance activities rarely encompass only technical issues. Managerial, social, financial, and institutional issues also play roles in advancing infrastructure sustainability. In too many cases, operations and maintenance are planned for only after a project has been completed.

The findings from this study suggest a lack of proper maintenance of boreholes, shallow wells, tap stands, and valley tanks. This is due in part to lack of spare parts, as well as inadequate or simply high prices of repairs that communities cannot afford. There is also a difficulty in finding well-trained technicians. Power shortages and lack of fuel to run generators also play a role. Other factors, including limited interactions training for hand pump mechanics at the local level and limited interactions with district water offices, also play a role (a district officer complained that *"hand pump mechanics have limited capacities and operate as segregated individuals"*). When facilities break down, repairs are often beyond the communities' capacity.

In Kotido, one community has not had functioning water taps for three years because pipes were cut. Another community in Bugiri had a spring, and when pipes were installed, the water stopped coming, and now seeps through the basement of the spring, gathering as pond water—this is now the water we use in this community. In Bundibugyo District, most piped water facilities are nonfunctional. Out of 13 boreholes drilled in Kisoro District, only one is operational. In Kalangala, the community's water sources included a shallow well, a water tank, seasonal ponds, and the lake. The preferred source of water is the shallow well, but when the team visited, it had broken down for two weeks and households were using the lake instead. As a resident explained: *"This community is only connected to piped water, and has no other source. But the piped water according to community members is not reliable. The reservoir tank is small and cannot satisfy the demand. So many times the water is not available in this community, and the demand for water has increased due to upcoming hotels and beaches, lodges."*

In another village visited for the fieldwork, the community had six tap stands in 2008, but because of poor workmanship and usage of small pipes coupled with low pressure the tap stands did not last for three months. In another community, the only functional tap located at the health center was not reliable because the water is always on and off, and the other three available taps had broken down years ago. A community in Kampala district had eight prepaid taps, but because of advanced technology used, they did not last and could not be repaired once they broke down (this would have required costly spare parts from South Africa). In one of the communities in Moyo District, some households bought water from kiosks, but supply sometimes is available only for one hour per day and water may be cut off for two days in a week. The availability of fuel for pumping determines the quantity and frequency of water available from taps, with hotels and eating places in the Town Council using a lot of the available water. These businesses also hire people to collect water from boreholes located far away, which is expensive. In a village in that district, the peak waiting time to get water was one hour because of a nonfunctional borehole. In another village, two boreholes were available, but one stopped being functional four years ago, and the remaining one was so hard to pump that in servicing the pump the mechanic's fingers were cut off. Many resorted to collecting water from swamps two kilometers away.

As district officers from two different districts explained: *"The district has 20 valley tanks, although very few (four) are still in good condition. Most of them have been vandalized and abandoned due to negligence by communities. The few dams that are still in good conditions are a result of good community participation as well as the effectiveness of water committees which were selected in those communities"*; *"The valley tanks dry up during the dry season which creates tension and conflict among the community members and cattle keepers. Most of valley tanks are poorly maintained and most of them are no longer functional."*

Responsibility

Perception as to who is responsible for providing clean and safe water vary between communities. Responses in focus groups ranged from the central government to local governments, community leaders, nongovernmental organizations (NGOs) operating in the community, and people themselves.

In Rutunda and Kanyanya (Kampala), access to clean and safe water was deemed a responsibility of the central government and the National Water and Sewerage Corporation. In some other areas as well, government is seen as *"solely responsible for keeping its citizens safe."* In Kamwokya, Kifumbira Zone in Kampala, people assumed it to be a human right requirement for the government to see that all people get safe water. This was a radical formulation. In Kalangala, the provision of water was seen as the responsibility of the government with an elderly woman explaining that *"since government has put a straw in people's resources through taxing then they should provide us with adequate and safe water."* In another urban area, community members suggested that it was also the responsibility of leaders such as members of parliament and district authorities to make sure that communities have clean and safe water since individual families cannot afford what it costs to get drilling machines for dams or boreholes. In rural areas as well, the government was seen as responsible for providing equipment and drilling machines necessary for constructing boreholes since community members cannot afford the cost.

At the same time, beyond central and district responsibilities, in many rural communities whenever there is a breakdown in the supply of water, the community is mobilized to make sure that repairs are done. In one village community, all members agreed that it was their responsibility to see that they access clean and safe water because it all begins at home. Communities in Kiboga District also thought that it is the responsibility of community members to see that they access clean and safe water, since they are the first ones to be victims of disease related to using unclean and unsafe water. In Kalangala as well, it was seen as the responsibility of community members to keep the water source clean by avoiding activities contaminate the water and boiling drinking water so that they can have safe water. But the district was also seen as responsible through bringing water nearer to the community, since communities do not have the capacity to connect water because of the advanced technologies involved, as well as costs. The district was seen as responsible for providing tanks and pumps and digging more shallow wells.

Local leaders were also deemed responsible to see that they work as a voice for the community and pass on the community's request and demands to those concerned so that they can intervene in circumstances of water shortages. Finally, in some areas, NGOs were also reported by members as being equally responsible in providing water tanks to communities with challenges in accessing water at low cost. For example, in Kiboga District, people said it was the responsibility of NGOs to provide access to clean and safe water. Overall, as recognized, for example, by communities in Kisoro, the responsibility of making sure that there is access to safe water appears to be multidimensional, with some roles to be played at central and district government levels, and other roles to be played at the level of communities and indeed households. Health inspectors, town clerks, mayors, and other individuals can also contribute, as can households, since it is often the case that households must pay fees to use water sources such as community wells, boreholes, or taps. Under normal circumstances, a jerry can of water from some of these sources could cost U Sh 200 to U Sh 300, but prices rise when water is in short supply, especially when water vendors provide the water to households during the dry seasons.

Clearly, communities have a role to play in the management of water sources, especially to ensure functionality. But this is not necessarily easy to achieve. It was mentioned in the previous section that only about half of Water Source Committees are functioning properly. Stronger community participation is important to avoid such issues. Committees of users (ideally gender balanced) can organize responsibility for the operation and maintenance of water systems. In the districts visited, some respondents noted that they had adopted community-based maintenance systems and had active water user committees, but because of their voluntary character they became nonfunctional. And in urban areas, few have heard of water user committees.

Communities with committed members on the water committee tend to have better accountability systems in place, and thereby better water systems with community members willing to contribute toward maintenance and operational costs. As a woman in Kiboga district explained: *"The borehole in our community has a water user committee which is functional. The water at the borehole is available most of the time and this is attributed to the functional and strong user committee that maintains it well."* Similarly, a man in Atopi village noted: *"At the functional borehole, we pay 1000 Shillings per month and as community members we feel the fee is affordable to most of us. We pay this money to the secretary for Finance on the water user committee. This committee has nine members, four of which are women. They make sure that the water source is secure and that the borehole is fenced. They supervise cleanliness around the borehole and fine those who do not follow the rules and regulations governing the borehole, and direct those with very dirty vessels to wash them before filling them with water to take home."*

On the other hand, some communities have failed to set up committees because of lack of community participation and willingness of community members to contribute toward operation and maintenance costs. The following quotes from focus group participants illustrate the issues: *"The initial water user committee that was elected to take charge of the water sources lost interest and disappeared. To members this committee was completely not functional. Some female members on the committee got married and left while others just left the area for greener pastures elsewhere"; "There was resistance from the community members to pay for the repairs. People are tired of contributing for shallow well repairs since the well keeps breaking down yet there are other communal contributions which are required monthly. For instance, every household is supposed to pay U Sh 1,000 whenever there is a breakdown but since this has become repetitive, people are now tiered of contributing"; "There is a water user committee at the dam with 14 chairpersons from 14 villages that make up the parish. The committee does not participate fully to the maintenance of the water source since many live far from it. The two who live nearby are left with all the work. It's only in dry seasons that committee members appear."*

The cost of operation and maintenance that communities have to pay in order to ensure the sustainability of their water sources came up repeatedly. Examples of costs mentioned by respondents are as follows: *"At the dam a caretaker is employed to make sure that no animals drink from the source. This same person helps in maintaining the water by removing silt and mud from the dam and whoever goes to collect water is required to carry five baskets of silt and mud, short of which one must pay U Sh 500 as a contribution to the caretaker. This person is paid U Sh 50,000 monthly and is normally employed during dry seasons"; "Members have to pay a quarterly fee of U Sh 1,000 per household for maintenance and in case of breakdown. This payment is done through the care taker who is the health center in-charge. In case one fails to pay for the water then she/he has no choice but to be stopped from getting this water and his/her alternative is to go to the stream water"; "At the only functional borehole, we pay U Sh 1,000 per month. Most feel the fee is affordable for community members. We pay this money to the secretary for Finance on the water user committee."* In many cases, the costs to be paid for access to these sources of water seem affordable, yet some are not willing or able to afford them.

In some areas, initiatives are undertaken to ensure that water sources are properly maintained. In Moyo, the District Council has approved bye laws on water and sanitation. Monies collected by users of boreholes must be banked with the Savings and Credit Cooperative Organizations (SACCOS) and Village Loan and

Savings groups. It is envisaged that this will help ensure proper management and accountability and to use the funds for loans to community members in times of distress. The funds will also be used when they are needed to buy spares for the boreholes if collections are not adequate to offset the cost of the spares.

As mentioned, in most urban places visited, water user committees are unheard of. The custody of the water points or sources is left to frequent users or owners of the land where they are located. Often protected springs and taps are maintained by water vendors or owners of the land, who earn a living from them. But difficulties arise, which then must be resolved by LC1 committees: *"This shallow well doesn't have a water user community but it's being taken care of by the LC1 executive of the village since the water user committee that was initially selected became ineffective. Contributions for O&M is only done by the fishing community at the landing site, yet other members from the village get water from the shallow well, and this is a disturbing issue to the fishing community"; "Water from the protected spring is free of charge. It's under the supervision of the LC1 committee but no water user committee has been elected to take care of the spring. Day to day cleaning is done by water vendors. This has created some tension between the vendors and community members who think that vendors don't allow other people to get water when their jerry cans are not yet filled. It becomes worse when water from other water sources are off. In such situations the committee has to come and calm things."*

Scarcity

While lack of functionality and local responsibility contributes to the scarcity of safe water in some areas, the simple issue of water scarcity is prominent in other areas. In Masindi district, water points accessed by one of the communities were located outside the community, with children crossing over a busy and dangerous highway to get water. In a site in Sembabule District, the water sources were concentrated on the upper side of the community, forcing residents to walk 2 kilometers to get water. The district dug four shallow wells but three broke down within a period of three weeks. Ditches and swamps in the area supplement the community with some water during the rainy season, but dry up in the hot season. Water is also collected from open ditches or ponds dug to water animals, with the alternative being an 18 kilometers walk to valley dams.

In Bundibugyo District, the officer in charge of water explained that *"the water sources are not enough in the villages. After people were resettled from the camps to their villages most NGOs withdrew their support so there is need for action by the district."* In Kiboga district, most areas have few natural springs that facilitate the construction of boreholes or shallow wells. In Kisoro District near mountain Muhavura, the only natural spring accessible to the community is shared by several villages. Although the spring is available throughout the year, collecting water has to be done with a cup to fill jerry cans or other containers. A communal water tank of 30,000 liters supplements the spring during the dry season, but at that time some households must move to the national park to collect water despite the long distance travelled and the risks involved.

In another village with more than 700 people, water is provided by two ponds, one private shallow well and one seasonal spring. Only eight households have piped water. The residents of this community lamented, *"We have no source of clean and safe water in our community. You can wonder whether we are cows, or whether we have leaders whom we voted for; they have drilled in three different sites and they claim they cannot find enough water for a borehole to function."* In one of the districts, water scarcity is so acute that and even dirty water in ponds is considered precious and struggled for. Ponds with green algae are used for domestic use. The scarcity of water explains and reinforces the scarcity of sanitation in the district. The health center has a borehole from which some community members get water, but the majority drink water from River Nile and many have been affected by a cholera outbreak. A tap water project was started in 2009 and now relies on solar power, which is cheaper, but coverage is low.

As already mentioned, seasonality plays a role in water scarcity in many districts. Uganda enjoys a tropical climate with two dry seasons from December to February and from June to August. During the dry seasons, many areas face shortages of water because of lack of natural springs, with the problem being most severe in cattle keeping corridors where people have to share water with animals. A respondent in Apac explained: *"During the dry season, there is no water at the only functional borehole. Everyone in the community resorts to the river, which is shared with animals. People wash their clothes, and bicycles and motorcycles in the river."* In Kisoro district, some households have access to piped water from the NWSC, but the water is on and off during the dry seasons because of low pressure. In that case, households must walk 4 kilometers to a spring. When the power goes off, the price of jerry cans from water vendors increases dramatically. Those who cannot afford high water prices must rely on alternative sources that tend to be located far away and may be contaminated. Sembabule district also suffers during the dry seasons as water sources in many communities dry up and the water in the valley dams and human-made ponds evaporates. This is sometimes averted by leaving the green cover to grow on the water to minimize evaporation. Some must then buy water from vendors, who collect it in trucks from as far as 20 kilometers away, with jerry cans then costing U Sh 1,000.

Water Quality

Safe Water

The preceding section makes it clear that lack of functionality, lack of local responsibility, and water scarcity may force households to rely on water of poor quality. Communities understand the risks associated with water of poor quality, and they have clear views as to what characterizes safe water. In Bundibugyo, the community considers as safe water obtained from a well-protected spring and fetched in a clean container. Some suggested that for water to be considered safe, it must be boiled, especially when the water is meant for drinking, since there are so many ways through which people may contaminate previously safe water, for example through poor storage. The available water points plotted on the community map were not considered safe, especially in the case of water from the open source flowing stream since it is being shared with animals. In other villages as well, only boiled water was considered safe, regardless of the source, because of an agreement that water may contain microorganisms that cannot be seen by the naked eye. In some urban areas as well, community participants noted that it is not easy to know with open eyes whether water is safe or not and the only solution is to boil. As a religious leader said in the discussion, *"It is not easy to measure the safety of water because most of us think that piped water and rain harvested water is safe water which may not be true."*

Similarly, in a village in Masindi, people considered boiled water as the only safe and clean water that would be ideal for drinking. A few women also considered rain-harvested water as safe and clean without any contamination. In another village, the two water points plotted on the village map were not considered safe and water flows from the hilly grounds collecting in the dam had lots of visibly dirty substances (feces, polythene bags, mud). All agreed that when water is stagnant this makes it even more unsafe. However, despite the fact that many considered only boiled water as being clean and safe, few in a number of communities reported taking the time to actually boil drinking water, especially when the water came from pipes, boreholes, and shallow wells which tended to be considered as free from germs, simply because the water came from underground sources perceived to have been filtered naturally through layers of soil.

In Karamoja region in the extreme north east arid zone, water quality issues were not as salient because availability itself was very low, and this was the more pressing issue. People were first concerned about getting whatever little water they could get. Typhoid was common and assumed to be caused by contaminated water: *"We have no chemical agents to test the water and confirm contamination. There are even fears that because typhoid cases are recurrent, they may lead to misdiagnosis to the effect that some people are HIV positive,"* a man conjectured. In another Karamoja region with acute water stress, the view was also expressed that with acute water scarcity in the district, all water, even dirty water from muddy ponds, is too precious to loose.

In many urban areas, tests are done about the quality of the water, but not everything can be tested. As a district water officer explained: *"We do quarterly checks on water sources and places which sell cooked food eaten by people in the urban areas. Some of the contamination was discovered to come from the dirty containers that are used to fetch and store the water. The district water office is mandated to undertake tests for bacterial contamination, but we do not have the kit to test for the presence of dissolved minerals in the water. This is done at the Ministry of Water and Environment. Complaints have been submitted by residents on the color of the water from two boreholes. When collected, the water was clear, but later its color changed. It was also reported that when it rains, there are living organisms detected in the borehole water. On piped tap water, there have been complaints on silt observed in the water. A sample of the water that changes color was picked by the Water*

Resources Departmental staff of MWE and taken to Kampala. No report on the results has been submitted to date from them."

In Moyo, complaints about water quality are directed to the Town Council, which forwards them to the District water office. At the peak of the cholera epidemic, WHO provided kits for testing, but the kits were expensive and only a few were available. A woman who participated in the focus groups noted the difficulty for the community to ascertain the safety of the water: *"We cannot determine if the water is clean or not. We do not even get feedback from the tests carried out by the water office. But the fact that some boreholes have been closed means there is a big problem with some of the water sources in this area."* The NWSC area manager in Apac also noted that while water quality is monitored and tested on a regular basis, testing for mineral contamination is only done by the ministry in Kampala. The testing kits at district water departments can only detect nonmineral contamination, particularly from feces.

When contamination is confirmed, a water source is condemned and people are advised not to use it. In Bugiri district, eastern Uganda, the health assistant and assistant water engineer also explained that water quality tests are done quarterly. In cases of contamination that may not be such serious threats, users are advised to boil the water before drinking, or to use that water for nondrinking purposes in the home. But users find it difficult to comply with such advice, for example to stop using a water source within their community because there are few alternatives. There are also challenges in convincing users that water may be unsafe, especially when the water appears colorless, which many take as an indicator of quality.

Community practices may undermine the quality of the water. In Bugiri, there have been complaints of worms seen in the water. But the biggest challenge is that people privately sink shallow wells in their homes and scoop the water out. These wells are called "shadoufs" after a similar technology used in the Arab Republic of Egypt to put water in canals for irrigation. Sometimes the shadoufs are near toilets. People do not know that sinking a water source requires a permit and regular inspection of the quality of the water. Using private water sources for commercial purposes is also subject to guidelines on rates that can be charged, but this is not enforced, and nobody bothers to acquire permits. In another community in Bugiri, a man lamented: *"If we ever manage to get a water source, we shall have been redeemed from the filthy water that we drink in this community; we use the muddy water the way it is. There are even some living organisms in the water. To illustrate how forgotten and desperate we are, even we Muslims who are aware that pigs swim and wash in this water, we have no option but to use it."*

In Masindi, the safety of water was doubted by the community because water sources were surrounded by overpopulated settlements, with schools and their latrines located around the same water sources and streams. For piped water, residents said that it turns brown, suggesting that it has been mixed up with running water during the rainy seasons. The many cases of diarrhea and typhoid in the community were taken as evidence that the water was not safe at all. In

Kalangala in Lake Victoria, community members also considered the water as unsafe because of old storage facilities: *"The reservoir tank was made out of steel so it must have rusted because the water from the tap is usually rusty especially in the morning."* The source of the piped water was also worrying, with old and rusty pipes together with human and animal activity around the source (when the team visited the source, cow dung was all over the place). Spring water was also not considered safe because animals drink from the same springs, since they are not secured with a fence. In addition, toilets were built near the water sources in part because of a lack of organization and monitoring (the area has no active water user committee). Some community members bathe at these protected springs. Respondents explained that community mobilization had weakened when piped water was introduced in 2002, as many households that would have had an interest in protecting the springs were now connected and thereby more relaxed.

In Lamwo on the northern border with Southern Sudan, people said good water is from surroundings that are clean, stressing that the source should not be near a toilet. But some beliefs may not be correct, as in the case of a man who argued: *"The water at the river is too cold to allow the survival of whatever germs it may have carried. Since time immemorial, people have been drinking the river water and no one has ever fallen sick or died because of taking this water in its natural form. Since the water is flowing, it carries away whatever dirt may have contaminated it."* At the same time, the fact that in that instance the water originates from underground springs on the top of Lamwo mountain helps in ensuring a higher level of purity.

When boiling water, some respondents mentioned that the boiling saucepan may turn black, showing that the water is not safe. In focus group discussions, people mentioned using methods like boiling, water guard, filtering, and solar disinfecting to make water safe. But there are costs involved, whether to buy charcoal for boiling water, or water guard. Buying clean storage containers is also costly, and many may not be able to, ending up using unclean and unsafe water. Even in Kifumbira, a suburb of the capital city where the water may look clean, residents noted that the water may not be safe as tests indicated high levels of contamination with fecal matter: *"To make the matters worse, even piped water which we assumed safe was found contaminated due to rusted lead pipes, coupled with human activities around the sources."* In Rutunda zone also in Kampala, people were unequivocal that for water to be considered as safe and clean it must be boiled. Residents considered water sources to be unsafe because most were located close to pit latrines. Besides, the commonly used protected spring was in a dilapidated condition. However, because of nonfunctionality of other water sources, members stated that they had no choice but to use this water despite their certain knowledge of it being unsafe.

Affordability and Culture

Residents are aware of the risk of unsafe water. In Rutunda zone, residents knew about diseases such as diarrhea, typhoid, bilharzia, and cholera that can be caused by unsafe water. But this awareness does not always translate into appropriate responses to improve the quality of water before using it. In Bukedea, the community used water from ponds without boiling it. After some members became sick with typhoid and had to spend substantial funds at the private clinic, they started boiling the water, but after some time, they went back to drinking the water without boiling it. In other communities as well, members know that children get sick of diarrhea because of unsafe water. In Bundibugyo, typhoid, diarrhea, gonorrhea, and cholera were all mentioned as resulting from contaminated water, leading to death in some cases. In Sembabule urban, a woman explained that *"there is a threat of contracting bilhazia due to use of dirty water which is mixed with both animal and human waste."* In Kisoro, members noted that because of the sharing of water with animals, there had been an infection by worms that affects the gum, and the moment this worm goes beyond the gullet the only alternative is a hospital operation.

What steps are residents taking to improve their water sources? The responses suggest a broad range of initiatives, but some also feel helpless. In Masindi, only a few households boiled the water because of the cost involved. A sack of charcoal costs depending on the location U Sh 20,000 to U Sh 40,000, and a small bundle of wood costs U Sh 2,000. A man explained that *"households can use six jerry cans of water a day at a total cost of U Sh 1200, making it hard to look for extra money for buying charcoal or firewood, so one may end up drinking the water without boiling it."* Some households use water guard, a chemical purifier, but many find its smell repulsive in drinking water, and water guard is also not always available. As a woman explained, *"only pregnant mothers were given water guard at the health centre, so many of us do boil water."*

In Kisoro, costs of buying charcoal, firewood, and bigger containers for storage were also mentioned. Apart from boiling, solar disinfection was also used as remedy, with some households simply leaving the water to settle in containers for a while. Even when the water is boiled, residents noted a bad smell because of the contamination of cow dung which may not disappear entirely. In Bundibugyo, despite agreeing that the water used by the community is not safe, most people conceded that they do not boil the water. In Kiboga district, an intensive community sensitization led to more residents boiling the water, but many still did not. Clorine is added in some areas to the water: *"Samples of water were tested from the tap and 20 percent had fecal matter contamination, so a higher dosage of chlorine was added at the source."*

Apart from cost, cultural practices also limit safe practices. In Kiboga community members agreed that water is made safe by boiling it or using water guard. Yet respondents explained that *"you know, many if not all of us grew up in rural areas and the days before there was adequate land so homestead were sparsely located and disease outbreaks were rare due to limited human activities near water sources, so even when we come to towns we forget that the water sources are contaminated by human activities and that areas are much congested."* In some areas, for example in Kalangala, some simply believe that water that looks clean can be assumed to be safe, and that piped water does not need to be boiled. In

Bundibugyo, residents said that they grew up knowing that all underground water, especially from springs, was perfectly safe, even for direct consumption. Others said that when water is boiled, its taste changes and becomes tasteless. Others viewed piped water as safe for any use. Elsewhere a woman explained: "*I am about 57 years old and I have been living on un-boiled water without falling sick, what matters to us is the government to extent gravity water points to us but not to tell us to boil the water.*"

In many areas, most people especially those of an advanced age, don't boil the water: "*We used to take water that was almost dirty from ditches and dams, we therefore feel that water from boreholes is very ok for us,*" an old man narrated. "*Our life span used to be longer than nowadays,*" he added. Some homes especially those with school-age children use water guard since it is supplied to children at school free of charge. But again, in most cases, little is done, as noted by a man in Lamwo district: "*We do nothing to this water. We do not boil, filter or leave it to settle. We are even aware it can cause diseases. We do not have filtering equipment to improve this water. We do not have time to boil this water because of the demanding household chores. We feel it is a waste of time since this water looks clean.*" A woman from the same area added: "*The water is shared with cattle. We are aware this water is bad, but we do not have time and fuel for boiling it, and we use it the way it is … Those who would have wanted to improve it say they are constrained by time, lack of saucepans for boiling it, and pots that take a long time to bring the water to boiling point. And firewood has become scarce over time.*"

This was echoed in Bukedea district: "*We have large families (some with 20 people) and this would require boiling a lot of water everyday*"; "*we have very small saucepans and pots and boiling water for many people is hard for us*"; or "*we are too tired after working in the gardens and cannot wait for the water to cool if it is boiled.*" Finally, in Amudat district where most respondents also did not improve the water and used the water as it is, the main reasons invoked for doing so were that "*we believe we have developed very high immunity to water diseases because we have used the dirty water for a very long time*" and "*we do not boil the water because they do not have time to wait for it to cool when they come back from gardens.*"

Finally, it is important to reiterate the fact that fetching water has an opportunity cost for households, especially for children and women, who are responsible for this chore. Respondents agreed that women, but even more so children, have this responsibility: "*It's the woman who suffers with water and that's why we don't expect her to travel for a long distance looking for water and boiling it as well since she has other domestic chores awaiting for her.*" Distance to water sources is a crucial factor in determining whether households get clean water. A water source near the dwellings of community members is often preferred even if it is less safe than another source farther away. In extreme cases, as in Sembabule, water scarcity forces residents to walk 18 kilometers to go and collect water where the tanks and valley dams are available.

In addition to walking time, waiting time is common. Where water is scarce, congestion may lead to chaos and fighting at the water sources, and instances of abuse of children and wives were reported, as when men beat their wife for delays at the water sources. In a village, the following comments were made: *"There are few public taps available in the community and only one outside the community, there is a lot of congestion making hard to access water without waiting for a period of one to two hours"*; *"At the shallow well, in the dry season the water is very little and after pumping five jerry cans one needs to wait for another 30 minutes."*

Conclusion

This chapter provided a detailed qualitative analysis of some of the challenges and constraints faced by households in accessing safe water—as well as some of their ongoing efforts to improve water sources in their communities. After a brief description of the methodology adopted for the qualitative fieldwork, the discussion of the data collected through focus groups and key informant interviews was organized along two thematic issues: the availability and quality of available water, as well as the measures that households and communities could take, but may often not be able to take, to improve availability and quality.

The factors that contribute to a lack of availability of water in many communities were analyzed along three dimensions: lack of functionality, lack of responsibility, and scarcity. Lack of functionality refers to the fact that in many communities existing water facilities are not working properly, whether this is due to (among others) aging systems, poor maintenance, or the inability to implement necessary repairs to broken-down equipment because of affordability or other constraints. Lack of local responsibility refers to poor organization or leadership at the local level that prevents communities from making necessary investments in improving water supply and leads to poor maintenance and a lack of incentives for households to keep water sources clean. Scarcity of water refers to the fact that in some communities, water is simply not easily available—it is scarce and often has to be brought into the community from distant sources. All three factors play a role in reducing the access to safe water for households.

Factors that contribute to a lack of quality of the water used by households and communities were analyzed along two dimensions—the focus was first on the perceptions of what constitutes safe water and then on factors that lead households not to take necessary steps that would improve water quality. Regarding perceptions, most households and communities are well aware of what constitutes safe water. They recognize that boiling water may be needed to ensure safety. There is also wide recognition of the need to build latrines sufficiently far away from water sources. At the same time, the pressures of daily life and common practices come in the way, because of both affordability constraints and cultural factors. As an example of affordability constraints, buying charcoal or firewood to boil water may be too costly for some households. Lack of affordability is also related to the opportunity cost in terms of time of fetching water that may be safer, but located farther away from household dwellings. As for cultural factors, in some areas, perceptions that the population used to be fine in terms of health outcomes without having to protect its water sources may now lead to suboptimal outcomes when contamination risks have increased substantially because of population growth and other factors. For others, there may be a perception that water that looks clean can (erroneously) be assumed to be safe. Overall, the qualitative fieldwork suggests that the constraints faced by households are complex, requiring solutions that tend to be context- and community specific. This does not lead to cookie-cutter solutions, but is important to document precisely because of the variety of local circumstances.

Note

1. The paragraphs that follow on the benefits of qualitative research are adapted from Clert, Gacitua-Mario, and Wodon (2001).

References

Alderman, H., L. Elder, A. Goyal, A. Herforth, Y. T. Hoberg, A. Marini, J. Ruel-Bergeron, J. Saavedra, M. Shekar, and S. Tiwari. 2013. *Improving Nutrition through Multisectoral Approaches*. Washington, DC: World Bank.

Barungi, M., and I. Kasirye. 2011. *Cost-effectiveness of Water Interventions: The Case for Public-stand Pipes and Bore-holes in Reducing Diarrhea among Urban Children in Uganda*. Kampala, Uganda: Economic Policy Research Center.

Bbaale, E., and F. Buyinza. 2012. "Micro-analysis of Mother's Education and Child Mortality: Evidence from Uganda." *Journal of International Development* 24 (S1): S138–58.

Bhutta, Z., T. Ahmet, R. Black, S. Cousens, K. Dewey, E. Giugliani, B. Haider, B. Kirkwood, S. Morris, H. Sachdev, M. Shekar, and the Maternal and Child Undernutrition Study Group. 2008. "What Works? Interventions for Maternal and Child Undernutrition and Survival." *The Lancet* 371 (9610): 417–40.

Blackden, M., and Q. Wodon, eds. 2006. *Gender, Time Use, and Poverty*. Washington, DC: World Bank.

Cairncross, S., C. Hunt, S. Boisson, K. Bostoen, V. Curtis, I. Fung, and W. Schmidt. 2010. "Water, Sanitation and Hygiene for the Prevention of Diarrhea." *International Journal of Epidemiology* 39 (Suppl. 1): i193–205.

Clert, C., E. Gacitua-Mario, and Q. Wodon. 2001. "Combining Qualitative and Quantitative Methods for Policy Research on Poverty within a Social Exclusion Framework." In *Measurement and Meaning: Combining Quantitative and Qualitative Methods for the Analysis of Poverty and Social Exclusion in Latin America*, edited by E. Gacitua-Mario and Q. Wodon. World Bank Technical Paper No. 518, Washington, DC: World Bank.

Denboba, A., R. Sayre, Q. Wodon, L. Elder, L. Rawlings, and J. Lombardi. 2014. *Stepping up Early Childhood Development: Investing in Young Children with High Returns*. Washington, DC: World Bank.

Dillingham, R., and R. L. Guerrant. 2004. "Childhood Stunting: Measuring and Stemming the Staggering Costs of Inadequate Water and Sanitation." *Lancet* 363 (9403): 94–5.

Esrey, A. 1996. "Water, Waste, and Well-being: A Multi-country Study." *American Journal of Epidimiology* 143 (6): 608.

Esrey, S. A., J. B. Potash, L. Roberts, and C. Shiff. 1991. "Effects of Improved Water Supply and Sanitation on Ascariasis, Diarrhoea, Dracunculiasis, Hookworm Infection, Schistosomiasis, and Trachoma." *Bulletin of the World Health Organization* 69 (5): 609–21.

Fay, M., D. Leipziger, Q. Wodon, and T. Yepes. 2005. "Achieving Child-Health-Related Millennium Development Goals: The Role of Infrastructure." *World Development* 33 (8): 1267–84.

Hutton, G., and L. Haller. 2004. *Evaluation of the Costs and Benefits of Water and Sanitation Improvements at the Global Level.* Geneva: World Health Organization.

Jalan, J., and M. Ravallion. 2003. "Does Piped Water Reduce Diarrhea for Children in Rural India?" *Journal of Econometrics* 112: 153–73.

Kosek, M., C. Bern, and L. R. Guerrant. 2003. "The Global Burden of Diarrheal Disease, as Estimated from Studies Published between 1992 and 2000." *Bulletin of the World Health Organization* 81: 197–204.

Moe, L. C., and D. R. Rheingans. 2006. "Global Challenges in Water, Sanitation and Health." *Journal of Water and Health* 04 (Suppl.): 41–57.

Rijsberman, F., and A. P. Zwane. 2012. "Copenhagen Consensus 2012 Challenge Paper: Water and Sanitation." http://www.copenhagenconsensus.com.

Schuster-Wallace, J. C., I. V. Grover, Z. Adeel, U. Confalonieri, and S. Elliot. 2008. *Safe Water as the Key to Global Health.* Hamilton, Ontario: United Nations University International Network on Water.

Spears, D. 2013. "How Much International Variation in Child Height Can Sanitation Explain?" Policy Research Working Paper No. 6351, World Bank, Washington, DC.

Tsimpo, C., and Q. Wodon. 2017. *Residential Piped Water in Uganda.* Washington, DC: World Bank.

World Bank. 2010. *Water and Development: An Evaluation of World Bank Support, 1997–2007.* Washington, DC: World Bank.

Zwane, A. P., and M. Kremer. 2007. "What Works in Fighting Diarrheal Diseases in Developing Countries? A Critical Review." *World Bank Research Observer* 22 (1): 1–24.

PART 2

Sanitation

CHAPTER 5

Access to Sanitation: Quantitative Analysis

Clarence Tsimpo and Quentin Wodon

Introduction

This chapter provides a basic diagnostic of access to sanitation in Uganda on the basis of nationally representative household surveys, as well as a quantitative analysis of focus-group data. Summary statistics are first provided on trends in access to sanitation (especially toilet facilities, but also waste disposal, bathroom types, and access to hand-washing facilities). This is done according to the modalities available in survey questionnaires and more aggregated definitions from the Joint Monitoring Programme (JMP) for water and sanitation of the World Health Organization. Constraints to access to sanitation are then briefly discussed relying on the community modules of existing surveys. Finally, qualitative data on the constraints faced by households to adopt good hygiene practices and on household perceptions of public toilets are analyzed to provide a better understanding of some of the factors limiting access to sanitation.

Sanitation can be defined as the set of hygienic means of promoting health and reducing disease through the prevention of human contact with waste hazards. As is the case for access to improved or safe water sources, adequate sanitation is essential for a range of development outcomes, including child morbidity, malnutrition, and mortality (on links between water, sanitation, and health, see among others Barungi and Kasirye 2011; Bbaale and Buyinza 2012; Debnboba et al. 2014; Esrey et al. 1991; Esrey 1996; Kosek, Bern, and Guerrant 2003; Jalan and Ravallion 2003; Dillingham and Guerrant, 2004; Fay et al. 2005; Hutton and Haller 2004; Moe and Rheingans 2006; Zwane and Kremer 2007; Bhutta, Ahmet, and Black 2008; Cairncross, Hunt, and Boisson 2010; World Bank 2010; Alderman et al. 2013; Spears 2013).

For example, as noted in chapter 2, millions die from diarrheal diseases every year, and most of these deaths can be attributed to unsafe water, poor sanitation, and lack of hygiene. Access to clean water and sanitation could reduce diarrhea and waterborne diseases by 25 percent (Schuster-Wallace et al. 2008). Improper disposal of waste (including human and animal feces, solid waste, and domestic waste water) also causes health problems for children and adults. In principle, simple solutions such as latrines, septic tanks, and proper garbage collection or disposal, as well as good personal hygiene—especially hand washing with soap—can go a long way in promoting adequate sanitation, but may still be out of reach for many households.

In a similar way to what was done in chapter 2 for the analysis of access to safe water, this chapter provides a basic descriptive diagnostic of access to sanitation in Uganda using household surveys, as well as a quantitative analysis of focus-group data. Again as in chapter 2, three complementary sources of data are used for the analysis.

First, summary statistics on trends in access to various types of toilets are provided according to the detailed modalities available in the Uganda National Household Survey questionnaires, as well as in a more aggregated way following (for the survey year 2012/13) the definitions proposed by the Joint Monitoring Programme (JMP) for water and sanitation of the World Health Organization. Data are also available in the community module on the types of toilets used by households, with fairly similar results. The surveys are then used to look at the most common modes of waste disposal for households, the types of bathroom they use, and finally whether they have a hand-washing facility near the various types of toilets they use.

Second, a separate nationally representative panel survey provides in the community module of that survey information from community leaders about some of the main reasons for incomplete latrine/toilet coverage. The response options range from low household income, to negative attitudes toward sanitation, poor landscape or terrain, as well as poor soil type to build latrines, ignorance, and finally the fact that households may be tenants or have no land.

Third, another way to look at constraints faced by households and communities to gain access to improved sanitation consists in conducting a simple quantitative analysis of feedback received from communities through qualitative fieldwork. In chapter 6, data from this qualitative fieldwork are analyzed in details and organized along several thematic issues. In this chapter, part of the feedback provided by households in focus groups is visualized quantitatively on the basis of responses to two questions asked to focus-group participants, first about challenges associated with good hygiene practices and then about perceptions of public toilets.

The structure of the chapter is as follows. Section 2 discusses trends in access to sanitation, with data on toilets, waste disposal, bathrooms, and hand washing. Section 3 discusses some of the constraints faced by households and communities in getting access to improved sanitation and adopting good hygiene practices. A conclusion follows.

Trends in Access to Sanitation

This section discusses trends in access to sanitation using the last four rounds of the Uganda National Household Survey, with a focus on toilet facilities, waste disposal, and hand washing. In some cases, comparable data are available for all four survey years, while in other cases, data are available only for one or a few survey years, either because some questions were not asked in the surveys for the other years or because there may be comparability issues between surveys in terms of the modalities used in the household survey questionnaires.

Data on the types of toilets used by households are provided in table 5.1. In the 2012/13 survey, only 7.3 percent of households have a flush toilet or a ventilated improved pit (VIP) latrine. These facilities are as expected much more frequent among households in the top welfare quintile than among the poor—in part because they are concentrated in Kampala. These types of toilets are virtually inexistent in the four bottom quintiles, and remain the exception even in the top quintile. Most households rely on pit latrines, whether covered or not, with or without slabs, with some differences by area and quintile, but not necessarily large ones. The exception is that one in four households in the bottom quintile does not have any access to toilets and thereby relies on bushes, bags, buckets, or other means—a proportion substantially higher than in other quintiles.

Overall, in the 10 years separating the first household survey (implemented in 2002/03) and the last survey (for 2012/13), even though the categories in the questionnaire are not consistent over time, there seems to have been an improvement in the types of toilets used by households, but gains have been limited. This is illustrated in map 5.1, which provides a visualization of the share of households using no toilet at all in the various years. There has been a gain nationally in some of the regions, but in 2012/13 that proportion was still at 9.7 percent, nationally, versus 13.3 percent in 2002/03 (unfortunately, the surveys do not provide a clear trend over time in access to improved latrines as defined by JMP; this is discussed below).

One of the categories listed in table 5.1 is that of Eco-San toilets. These toilets involve the separation of urine from feces and recycling of human waste. As shown in table 4.1, less than 1 percent of households relied on those toilets in 2012/13 despite efforts to make them available among others by nongovernmental organizations (NGOs). The qualitative work in chapter 6 suggests that most people do not like these toilets because they are not easy to use and have proved rather difficult to maintain. Cultural factors such as the lack of use of water and the reliance on ashes also tend to reduce the reliance on the toilets, among others by Muslim populations.

Table 5.2 complements the data from the household module of the survey by providing data from community leaders on the types of toilets available in communities (multiple responses are allowed), as well as the approximate shares of households using various types of toilets in the communities. The findings are similar to those obtained with the household module, with most households relying on pit latrines, whether covered or not, with or without slabs (in the table, apart from columns based on location, communities are also ranked into three terciles of welfare according to the average level of consumption per equivalent

Table 5.1 Types of Toilet Used by Households

Percent

	Location			Region				Welfare quintile					Total
	Kampala	Other urban	Rural	Central	Eastern	Northern	Western	Q1	Q2	Q3	Q4	Q5	
2012/13													
Flush toilet	14.0	3.0	0.2	3.3	0.6	0.4	1.2	0.0	0.0	0.2	1.0	4.5	1.5
VIP latrine	22.4	12.6	2.6	12.6	2.7	1.7	4.2	0.7	1.7	2.7	5.1	13.7	5.8
Covered pit, with slab	32.8	32.8	13.5	29.5	19.8	8.2	12.6	9.0	11.0	14.8	20.0	30.3	18.6
Covered pit w/o slab	28.2	31.8	48.2	24.9	49.4	40.6	63.4	41.7	51.8	47.7	47.7	34.0	43.6
Uncovered pit, with slab	1.7	5.8	4.6	7.5	5.5	2.4	2.5	3.7	4.7	5.9	4.6	4.6	4.7
Uncovered pit, w/o slab	0.5	8.1	18.2	17.1	13.2	15.9	14.0	18.3	18.9	17.7	15.1	9.2	15.1
Ecosan (compost toilet)	0.0	1.0	0.9	0.4	0.7	2.1	0.7	1.6	1.0	0.5	1.2	0.5	0.9
No facility/bush/bags/and so on	0.2	5.0	11.8	4.8	8.2	28.7	1.5	24.9	10.9	10.5	5.3	3.2	9.7
Other	0.2	0.0	0.0	0.1	0.0	0.1	0.0	0.0	0.1	0.1	0.1	0.0	0.0
Total	100.0	100.0	100.0	100.0	100.0	100.0	100.0	100.0	100.0	100.0	100.0	100.0	100.0
2009/10													
Covered pit, private	8.0	19.1	41.6	30.7	34.3	26.7	54.9	34.9	42.7	39.5	39.1	29.9	36.6
Covered pit, shared	63.5	58.2	26.6	38.7	31.1	36.8	24.2	19.8	25.7	30.4	37.4	42.9	32.9
VIP latrine private	2.0	1.6	1.2	2.8	1.0	0.4	0.3	0.7	0.2	0.4	1.2	2.9	1.3
VIP latrine shared	7.9	6.2	1.4	5.3	0.9	1.5	0.9	0.2	0.9	0.8	1.5	6.2	2.4
Uncovered pit	3.2	5.1	18.3	15.2	20.2	9.3	16.3	20.0	20.1	19.9	15.9	7.5	15.7
Flush, private	11.9	6.7	0.3	4.8	0.6	0.3	0.6	0.0	0.0	0.1	0.1	6.6	1.9
Flush, shared	1.9	1.2	0.0	0.7	0.1	0.0	0.2	0.0	0.1	0.1	0.1	0.8	0.3
Bush	0.0	2.1	10.3	1.4	11.4	24.8	2.3	23.8	9.8	8.1	4.4	2.9	8.6
Other	1.6	0.0	0.4	0.5	0.6	0.3	0.4	0.7	0.5	0.7	0.3	0.2	0.4
Total	100.0	100.0	100.0	100.0	100.0	100.0	100.0	100.0	100.0	100.0	100.0	100.0	100.0

table continues next page

Table 5.1 Types of Toilet Used by Households *(continued)*

Percent

	Location			Region				Welfare quintile					Total
	Kampala	Other urban	Rural	Central	Eastern	Northern	Western	Q1	Q2	Q3	Q4	Q5	
2005/06													
Covered pit, private	20.9	26.8	44.3	39.2	37.9	20.6	61.3	28.1	40.3	46.3	46.7	40.2	40.8
Covered pit, shared	65.4	54.3	27.5	35.9	24.1	48.7	25.7	31.5	26.6	28.1	34.3	41.7	33.1
VIP latrine private	1.1	1.9	0.7	1.6	0.5	0.4	0.4	0.1	0.2	0.3	0.5	2.3	0.8
VIP latrine shared	3.2	4.5	1.2	2.6	0.7	2.8	0.5	1.4	1.5	0.6	0.9	3.5	1.7
Uncovered pit	0.3	4.6	13.9	14.2	19.6	6.2	6.5	15.2	16.7	13.9	11.7	5.0	11.9
Flush, private	5.7	2.1	0.1	1.9	0.4	0.1	0.2	0.0	0.0	0.0	0.0	3.0	0.8
Flush, shared	2.3	1.7	0.1	0.6	0.6	0.1	0.2	0.0	0.0	0.0	0.3	1.3	0.4
Bush	0.0	3.3	11.4	3.5	15.1	20.9	4.0	22.8	13.4	9.8	4.8	2.6	9.8
Other	1.0	0.8	0.8	0.6	1.2	0.4	1.2	0.9	1.2	0.9	0.8	0.4	0.8
Total	100.0	100.0	100.0	100.0	100.0	100.0	100.0	100.0	100.0	100.0	100.0	100.0	100.0
2002/03													
Covered pit, private	19.8	26.2	48.5	42.4	39.7	20.2	69.4	32.3	46.2	50.8	50.3	41.0	44.2
Covered pit, shared	65.6	54.1	22.1	33.5	23.9	36.8	19.9	19.3	23.3	22.9	28.8	40.9	28.3
VIP latrine private	0.8	1.7	1.1	2.0	0.7	0.7	0.9	0.1	0.8	0.9	1.0	2.2	1.1
VIP latrine shared	6.8	3.9	0.5	2.8	0.7	0.5	0.5	0.2	0.1	0.7	1.7	3.0	1.3
Uncovered pit	0.0	5.2	12.1	12.4	15.6	7.5	5.2	15.4	13.2	11.8	10.3	5.2	10.6
Flush, private	5.2	3.7	0.1	1.5	0.6	0.2	0.5	0.0	0.1	0.0	0.1	2.9	0.8
Flush, shared	1.5	2.6	0.0	0.4	0.5	0.2	0.3	0.0	0.0	0.1	0.3	1.1	0.4
Bush	0.0	2.3	15.0	4.2	17.1	33.5	3.4	31.6	16.2	12.1	7.0	3.3	12.7
Other	0.4	0.4	0.6	0.7	1.2	0.3	0.0	1.0	0.3	0.7	0.6	0.5	0.6
Total	100.0	100.0	100.0	100.0	100.0	100.0	100.0	100.0	100.0	100.0	100.0	100.0	100.0

Source: Data from Uganda UNHS surveys.

Map 5.1 Share of Households with No Toilet at All, 2002–13

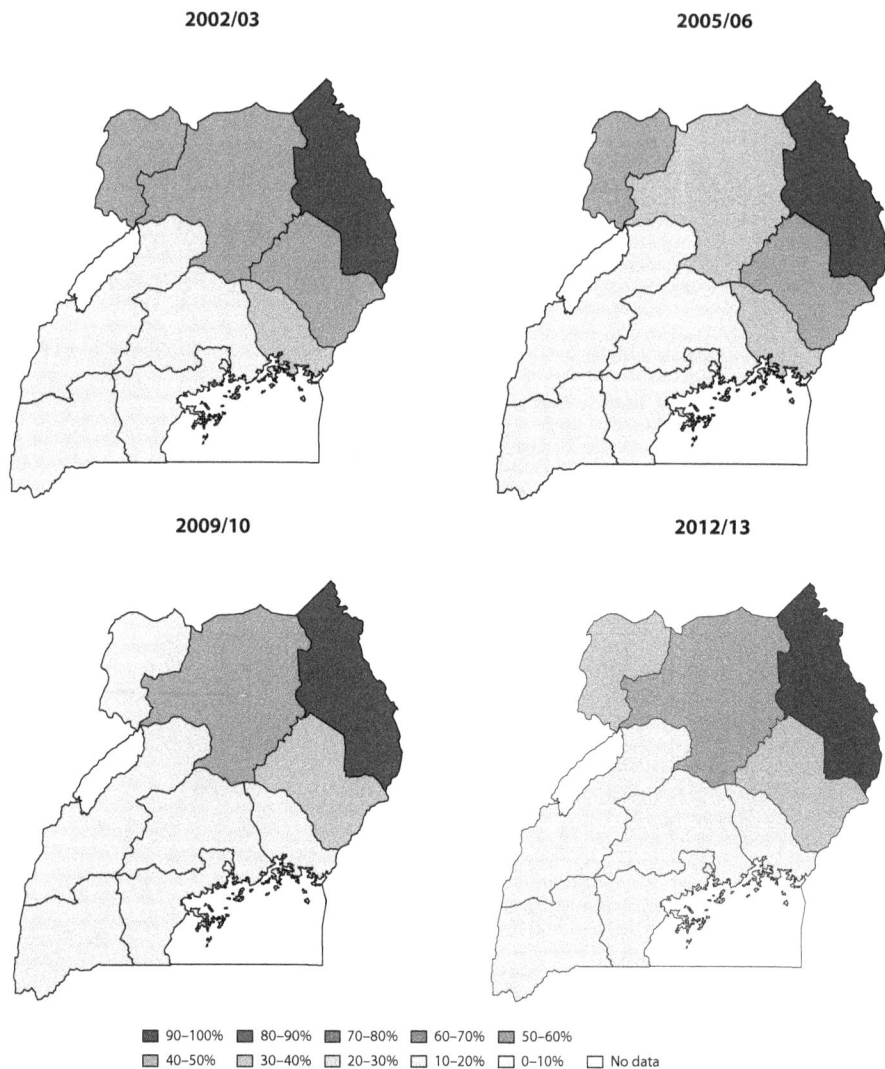

2002/03   2005/06

2009/10   2012/13

| ■ 90–100% | ■ 80–90% | ▨ 70–80% | ▨ 60–70% | ▨ 50–60% |
| ▨ 40–50% | ▨ 30–40% | □ 20–30% | □ 10–20% | □ 0–10% | □ No data |

Source: Data from 2002/03, 2005/06, 2009/10, and 2012/13 UNHS surveys.

adult of the households living in the communities, with consumption per equivalent adult measured in the household module).

Statistics on access to sanitation may also be presented in a more aggregated way. While different definitions of what constitutes improved sanitation are used in the literature, it is customary to rely on the definitions proposed by the JMP for water and sanitation of the World Health Organization. As noted in the introduction, according to the JMP, improved sanitation refers to flush toilets, piped sewer systems, septic tanks, flush/pour flush to pit latrines, ventilated improved pit latrines, pit latrines with slab, composting toilets, and what is referred to as special cases. Unimproved sanitation refers to flush/pour flush to

Table 5.2 Main Types of Toilet Used in Communities: Community Module, 2012/13

Percent

	Location			Region				Welfare tercile			
	Kampala	*Other urban*	*Rural*	*Central*	*Eastern*	*Northern*	*Western*	*T1*	*T2*	*T3*	*Total*
Availability of types of toilets in community [a]											
Covered latrine private	93.8	80.4	79.6	93.1	90.4	51.9	77.8	73.4	79.5	85.9	80.6
Covered latrine shared	83.3	60.0	67.2	55.8	74.7	58.3	78.3	71.7	64.8	64.2	66.5
VIP latrine private	44.6	31.4	27.4	47.7	15.8	13.3	34.1	20.3	29.3	35.0	29.2
VIP latrine shared	37.7	14.8	15.4	24.6	5.4	4.4	29.3	8.1	14.1	23.6	16.5
Uncovered pit latrine	55.4	34.4	35.8	66.4	27.7	25.1	17.1	32.1	34.4	41.0	36.6
Flush toilet private	10.6	14.0	9.9	10.2	2.4	4.1	27.4	4.6	9.0	16.1	10.8
Flush toilet shared	0.0	4.3	2.7	1.5	1.8	2.8	6.3	0.8	3.3	4.0	2.9
Ecosan toilet	0.0	1.9	1.3	0.6	0.4	0.0	4.7	0.0	3.2	0.9	1.3
No toilet/bush	46.5	51.3	49.5	66.5	53.7	52.3	20.5	51.7	48.9	48.9	49.7
Shares of households, by type of toilet											
Covered latrine private	33.5	39.7	39.5	40.9	43.9	29.2	40.4	36.5	41.5	39.5	39.2
Covered latrine shared	21.8	18.4	22.2	13.3	27.2	15.4	30.5	21.3	22.3	20.7	21.3
VIP latrine private	4.6	2.9	2.8	5.8	0.8	1.0	3.0	2.0	2.7	3.5	2.9
VIP latrine shared	7.5	4.0	2.1	3.4	1.2	0.6	5.8	1.4	2.1	4.2	2.8
Uncovered pit latrine	19.9	10.7	9.9	21.6	6.2	5.2	5.6	7.5	8.5	14.0	10.6
Flush toilet private	3.3	3.0	1.1	1.2	0.3	0.2	5.2	0.4	0.9	3.0	1.7
Flush toilet shared	0.0	0.6	0.7	0.1	0.1	1.9	0.8	0.3	1.3	0.5	0.6
Ecosan toilet	0.0	0.1	0.2	0.0	0.0	0.0	0.8	0.0	0.5	0.1	0.2
No toilet/bush	7.1	19.1	18.4	12.9	17.7	42.2	3.5	27.3	17.3	12.3	17.9

Source: Data for Uganda is from the 2012/13 UNHS survey.
Note: VIP = ventilated improved pit.
a. Multiple responses were possible.

elsewhere (not latrines), pit latrines without slabs, buckets, hanging toilets or latrines, and other modes of disposal. Typically, facilities that are shared are not considered as improved, but one may usefully distinguish among unimproved sanitation and improved but shared sanitation.

Table 5.3 Improved and Unimproved Toilet Facilities Used by Households

Percent

	Location			Region				Welfare quintile					Total
	Kampala	Other urban	Rural	Central	Eastern	Northern	Western	Q1	Q2	Q3	Q4	Q5	
Improved versus unimproved classification													
Improved	19.7	18.6	12.3	20.9	16.5	3.5	11.6	8.1	10.8	12.3	13.4	21.0	14.0
Unimproved	79.1	80.4	87.1	78.3	83.0	95.6	87.8	90.8	88.7	87.5	85.8	78.2	85.3
Other	1.2	1.0	0.6	0.9	0.4	0.9	0.6	1.1	0.5	0.3	0.7	0.9	0.7
Total	100.0	100.0	100.0	100.0	100.0	100.0	100.0	100.0	100.0	100.0	100.0	100.0	100.0
Improved, shared improved, and unimproved classification													
Improved	19.7	18.6	12.3	20.9	16.5	3.5	11.6	8.1	10.8	12.3	13.4	21.0	14.0
Shared improved	50.5	36.1	9.4	31.9	12.6	11.1	9.4	6.9	7.5	11.8	18.2	32.2	17.3
Unimproved	28.6	44.3	77.7	46.3	70.5	84.5	78.5	84.0	81.2	75.7	67.6	46.0	68.0
Other	1.2	1.0	0.6	0.9	0.4	0.9	0.6	1.1	0.5	0.3	0.7	0.9	0.7
Total	100.0	100.0	100.0	100.0	100.0	100.0	100.0	100.0	100.0	100.0	100.0	100.0	100.0

Source: Data from Uganda 2012/13 UNHS survey.

Table 5.3 provides estimates of the share of the population with access to improved sanitation based on these definition with the 2012/13 data (because of changes in questionnaire categories over time, it is difficult to provide a trend over time in these aggregate access measures). The data suggest that only 14 percent of households have access to improved sanitation. If unimproved facilities are split between shared but improved facilities and unimproved facilities, the proportion of households with a shared improved facility is 17.3 percent. Clearly, most households do not have access to adequate sanitation, and when they do have access, in most cases the facilities used are shared, often by many households. Map 5.2 provides a visualization of access rates to improved latrines by region.

Map 5.2 Share of Households Using an Improved Latrine, 2012/13

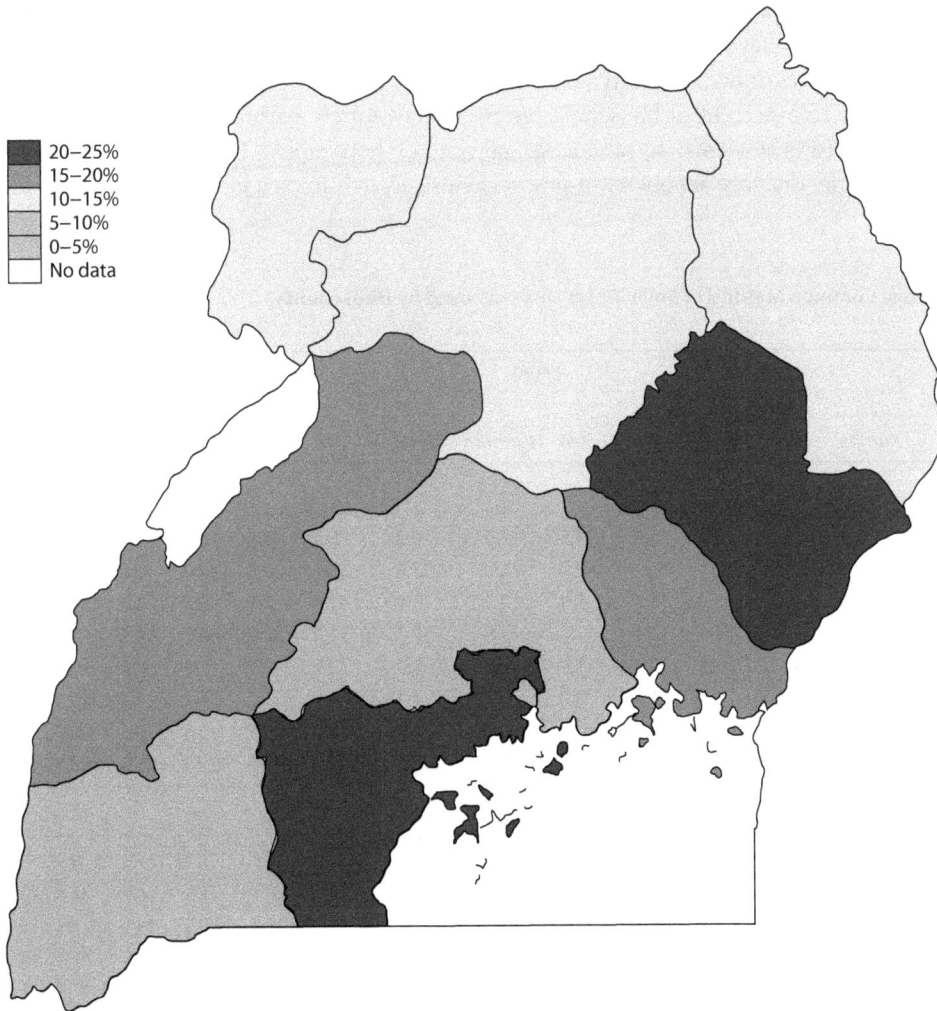

Source: Data from 2012/13 UNHS survey.

Overall, when including both improved and shared improved facilities, 31.3 percent of households have access to improved facilities. The estimates obtained with the 2012/13 Uganda National Household Survey are fairly similar to those obtained with the 2011 Demographic and Health Survey (DHS), according to which the corresponding share is 31.9 percent (although the DHS suggests a higher share of households with their own improved latrine, and a smaller shared with an improved shared latrine that is shared; the basic statistics are provided in annex).

Table 5.4 provides data on the most common modes of waste disposal used by households, while table 5.5 documents the types of bathrooms they rely upon. Gardens, pits, or heaps tend to be used most often for waste disposal, by respectively 43.4 percent, 31.8 percent, and 11.2 percent of households. Waste vendors are relied upon mostly in Kampala by close to half of the households living in the capital. Less than one household in ten uses a skip bin or burning. Skip bins and especially pits have become more common over time. In terms of bathrooms, makeshift structures or no bathroom at all are the most common occurrences, for 35.3 percent and 25.5 percent of households, respectively. Outside bathrooms (with or without drainage) are used by about 40 percent of households. Inside bathrooms with proper drainage are observed almost exclusively in Kampala for a fifth of households.

Table 5.4 Most Common Method of Solid Waste Disposal Used by Households
Percent

	Location			Region				Welfare quintile					
	Kampala	Other urban	Rural	Central	Eastern	Northern	Western	Q1	Q2	Q3	Q4	Q5	Total
					2012/13								
Skip bin	6.9	5.8	0.4	3.0	1.5	1.9	0.9	0.4	0.5	0.7	2.1	4.2	1.9
Pit	6.9	32.7	33.3	17.1	48.0	36.9	27.6	33.1	33.8	34.0	30.6	29.4	31.8
Heap	21.6	16.5	8.9	15.3	5.9	12.2	11.0	11.1	7.2	9.7	11.0	14.7	11.2
Garden	3.3	25.4	51.5	37.4	42.2	45.8	50.3	51.2	53.5	48.2	44.6	28.7	43.4
Burning	11.9	12.5	5.2	14.5	1.3	2.7	8.0	3.5	3.5	5.4	8.0	11.7	7.1
Waste vendor	47.8	6.6	0.3	11.7	0.9	0.2	1.2	0.4	1.0	1.2	3.0	10.5	4.0
Other	1.6	0.6	0.6	1.0	0.2	0.2	1.0	0.3	0.4	0.8	0.6	0.9	0.6
Total	100.0	100.0	100.0	100.0	100.0	100.0	100.0	100.0	100.0	100.0	100.0	100.0	100.0
					2002/03								
Skip bin	20.8	12.8	0.5	5.9	1.9	1.4	2.4	0.4	0.6	1.4	2.8	8.3	3.2
Pit	5.6	29.0	22.1	12.6	23.2	29.4	25.9	17.5	20.8	21.0	24.9	22.8	21.7
Heap	41.4	25.6	11.7	21.7	6.3	20.7	11.8	12.7	11.4	11.5	14.7	22.3	15.1
Garden	3.5	18.8	56.4	45.3	61.2	26.6	57.3	58.2	57.5	56.6	48.9	31.7	48.9
Burning	20.9	12.5	5.5	12.2	5.6	8.0	2.0	5.9	5.1	5.0	6.6	11.7	7.3
Other	7.9	1.3	3.9	2.3	1.8	13.9	0.6	5.4	4.7	4.5	2.3	3.2	3.9
Total	100.0	100.0	100.0	100.0	100.0	100.0	100.0	100.0	100.0	100.0	100.0	100.0	100.0

Source: Data from Uganda UNHS surveys.

Table 5.5 Types of Bathroom Used by Households

Percent

	Location			Region				Welfare quintile					Total
	Kampala	Other urban	Rural	Central	Eastern	Northern	Western	Q1	Q2	Q3	Q4	Q5	
2012/13													
Inside, with drainage	17.2	6.2	1.4	7.3	1.6	0.9	2.0	0.4	0.3	0.6	1.5	9.7	3.2
Inside, no drainage	2.0	1.9	1.0	2.4	0.4	0.4	1.3	0.2	0.3	1.8	1.0	2.1	1.2
Outside, with drainage	33.7	29.6	6.6	25.6	6.5	10.2	6.6	2.8	5.4	6.8	12.7	27.6	12.9
Outside, no drainage	34.5	24.9	19.9	19.8	36.4	20.2	8.7	20.7	20.6	23.5	21.4	21.9	21.7
Makeshift	4.0	21.7	41.5	22.1	35.4	29.7	56.8	34.3	43.5	40.8	40.2	23.6	35.3
None	8.6	15.6	29.5	22.7	19.6	38.4	24.5	41.1	29.9	26.4	23.2	15.0	25.5
Other	0.0	0.2	0.1	0.2	0.2	0.2	0.0	0.5	0.0	0.1	0.0	0.1	0.1
Total	100.0	100.0	100.0	100.0	100.0	100.0	100.0	100.0	100.0	100.0	100.0	100.0	100.0
2002/03													
Inside	18.7	10.9	2.6	10.0	2.3	1.3	2.5	0.6	0.9	1.8	4.1	11.9	4.6
Outside (built)	65.1	61.3	39.1	44.8	47.3	32.0	45.0	29.2	37.4	40.6	45.7	55.7	43.2
Outside (makeshift)	8.2	12.8	19.7	17.9	15.2	20.6	20.1	16.7	19.6	19.5	22.3	14.1	18.2
None	8.0	15.1	38.6	27.4	35.3	46.2	32.4	53.6	42.1	38.1	28.0	18.3	34.1
Total	100.0	100.0	100.0	100.0	100.0	100.0	100.0	100.0	100.0	100.0	100.0	100.0	100.0

Source: Data from Uganda UNHS surveys.

Finally, table 5.6 provides data on the availability of hand-washing facilities for households. Most households (85 percent) do not have a hand-washing facility, and among those who do, for half water is available, but not soap. The share of households declaring not having access to a hand-washing facility may actually have increased between 2009/10 and 2012/13, the two survey years for which that question is asked in the household questionnaire. Map 5.3 provides a

Table 5.6 Availability of Hand-Washing Facility for Households
Percent

	Location			Region				Welfare quintile					
	Kampala	Other urban	Rural	Central	Eastern	Northern	Western	Q1	Q2	Q3	Q4	Q5	Total
					2012/13								
No	82.2	80.2	86.8	80.0	84.2	93.2	87.0	93.0	89.5	87.7	84.5	77.8	85.0
Yes with water only	4.3	9.4	6.1	10.2	6.5	3.7	4.9	4.9	4.7	5.9	6.8	9.4	6.8
Yes with water and soap	11.9	9.3	6.2	9.1	8.0	2.0	7.3	1.8	4.9	5.4	7.3	11.9	7.2
Yes with no water	1.6	1.0	0.9	0.7	1.3	1.1	0.9	0.4	0.9	1.1	1.4	0.9	1.0
Total	100.0	100.0	100.0	100.0	100.0	100.0	100.0	100.0	100.0	100.0	100.0	100.0	100.0
					2009/10								
No	76.0	74.9	82.8	71.2	82.9	85.8	90.2	88.0	86.3	85.5	85.0	69.6	81.3
Yes with water only	9.3	11.8	10.3	13.4	9.6	12.8	5.7	8.7	9.6	10.1	8.9	13.1	10.4
Yes with water and soap	14.7	13.2	6.9	15.4	7.6	1.5	4.2	3.3	4.1	4.4	6.2	17.3	8.3
Total	100.0	100.0	100.0	100.0	100.0	100.0	100.0	100.0	100.0	100.0	100.0	100.0	100.0

Source: Data from Uganda UNHS surveys.

Map 5.3 Share of Households with Hand-Washing Facility with Water and Soap, 2009/10 and 2012/13

a. 2009/10   b. 2012/13

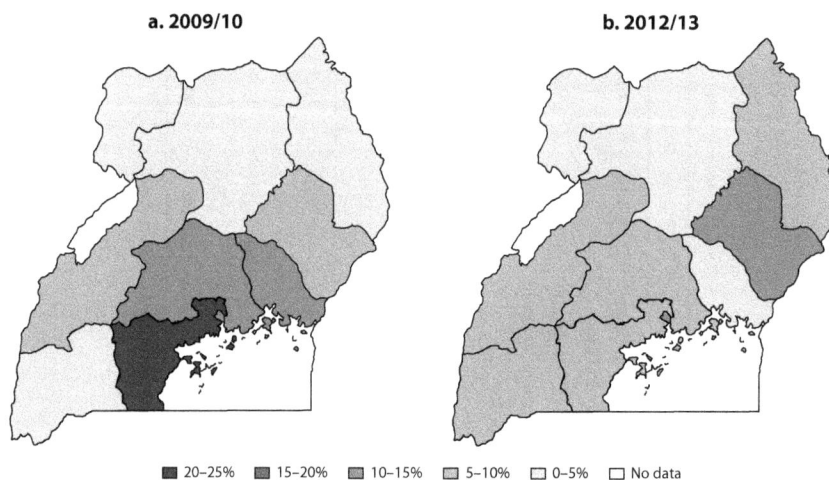

■ 20–25%   ■ 15–20%   ■ 10–15%   ▨ 5–10%   ☐ 0–5%   ☐ No data

Source: Data from 2009/10 and 2012/13 UNHS surveys.

visualization of the shares of households with hand-washing facilities (with water and soap) in the two survey years by region.

In the 2011 DHS, as shown in the annex, a larger share of households (29 percent) are documented as having a hand-washing facility, but among those, a smaller share are documented as having water and/or soap, so that when considering not only the availability of a facility but also the availability of water, soap, or both, the results are of the same order of magnitude.

Constraints for Access to Sanitation

The qualitative work in chapter 6 will provide a rich analysis of the constraints faced by households and communities to gain access to sanitation. But one question asked in a different survey—the 2010/11 Uganda National Panel Survey—already provides some insights. In the community module of that survey, information from community leaders is available on the reasons for incomplete latrine/toilet coverage in the community. The response options include low income, negative attitudes, poor landscape or terrain, as well as poor soil type to build latrines, ignorance, and finally the fact that households may be tenants or have no land.

As shown in table 5.7, community leaders believe that ignorance (in 38.4 percent of cases) and negative attitudes toward sanitation (in 18.1 percent of cases) are to blame in more than half the communities for incomplete latrine/toilet coverage. Low household income comes next (15.2 percent of cases), followed by poor landscape or terrain, poor soil type, or the lack of land (each for 6 to 7 percent of cases). There are differences between areas and by welfare levels in communities in the factors at work (for example, cost is mentioned more in Kampala), but with a few exceptions these differences are limited—suggesting

Table 5.7 Major Reason for Incomplete Latrine/Toilet Coverage—Community Module, 2010/11
Percent

	Location			Region				Welfare tercile			
	Kampala	Other urban	Rural	Central	Eastern	Northern	Western	T1	T2	T3	Total
Low income	25.5	12.2	15.4	17.4	19.6	6.6	11.3	18.1	12.4	15.1	15.2
Negative attitude	21.1	17.8	18.0	30.1	13	9.1	14.5	12.7	11.4	27.4	18.1
Poor landscape or terrain	5.1	6.6	7.6	6.6	6.1	9.0	9.9	4.9	6.9	9.4	7.3
Ignorance	42.5	40.3	37.6	31.7	37.6	53.1	31.8	44.3	45.0	28.8	38.4
Poor soil type	2.0	9.3	5.4	3.2	7.0	9.9	4.7	9.1	4.4	5.3	6.1
Tenants	0.0	2.4	1.6	1.5	1.8	0.0	5.7	0	2.3	2.5	1.7
No land	2.0	8.7	6.3	4.4	3.4	10.2	16.9	7.1	5.4	7.1	6.6
Other	1.8	2.7	8.2	5.2	11.6	2.1	5.2	3.8	12.2	4.5	6.7
Total	100.0	100.0	100.0	100.0	100.0	100.0	100.0	100.0	100.0	100.0	100.0

Source: Data from Uganda 2010/11 Panel survey.

that the three main factors of ignorance, negative attitudes, and low income are at work in many communities in the country.

Another way to look at the issue of the constraints faced by households and communities to gain access to improved and safe water sources consists in implementing a simple quantitative analysis of some of the feedback received from communities in the qualitative fieldwork. In the next chapter, detailed qualitative data from focus groups and key informants are organized along a number of thematic issues. In this chapter, it is useful to briefly summarize quantitatively and in a visual way some of the issues mentioned by households in the qualitative fieldwork.

This is done in figures 5.1 and 5.2 on the basis of a classification of responses from focus-group participants to two simple questions: the first question was on challenges associated with good hygiene practices: What limits people from practicing the known good hygiene practices in this community?; and the second question was on perceptions of public toilets: What are the ideas people have about public toilets in this community? The idea in the rapid empirical results provided here is not to conduct any in-depth analysis of the responses to those questions provided in focus groups (this is done in chapter 6), but to note some of the broad themes considered by respondents.

As visualized in figure 5.1, on the basis of a simple count of responses to the first question agreed to by focus groups, concerns related to attitudes and affordability dominate in both urban and rural areas, with issues of attitude seen as especially damaging to good hygienic practices in rural areas. In addition, ignorance, or possibly traditional behaviors as well as cultural norms, are also mentioned fairly often in rural areas while limited space (for example, to build adequate latrines) is more of a constraint mentioned by respondents in urban areas, as expected. These perceptions are fairly similar overall to the feedback provided by community leaders in the community module of the 2011/11 panel survey for which basic statistics were provided in table 5.7. In figure 5.2, perceptions of public toilets tend to be associated with the demand for separate sections for women and men, as well as for persons with disabilities.

Figure 5.1 Challenges Associated with Good Hygiene Practices

a. Urban   **b. Rural**

Source: Qualitative fieldwork in this study.

Figure 5.2 Perceptions about Public Toilets

a. Urban   b. Rural

Source: Qualitative fieldwork in this study.

The respondents also express a desire for higher levels of privacy in terms of location of these public toilets. Availability of water and soap was an absolute requirement noted for public toilets. But issues of maintenance and care-taking of public toilets, some of which may not be fully functional, are also mentioned.

Conclusion

The objective of this chapter was to provide a basic diagnostic of trends in access to adequate sanitation in Uganda on the basis of nationally representative household surveys and to discuss some of the constraints faced by households in benefitting from adequate sanitation, relying on both household survey data and some of the data collected through focus groups in qualitative fieldwork. The data suggest that only a small minority of households have access to improved sanitation, as defined by the JMP for water and sanitation of the World Health Organization. The broad landscape of the types of toilets, waste disposal techniques, bathrooms, and hand-washing practices observed in the country tends not to have changed much between the various household survey years which cover the last decade.

A number of constraints to access to sanitation can be identified in the surveys, as well as in qualitative fieldwork. Survey data from community leaders suggest that ignorance, negative attitudes, and lack of income are the main reasons for incomplete latrine/toilet coverage in communities. In addition, poor landscape or terrain, poor soil type, and a lack of land also play a significant role. The analysis of views among focus-group participants regarding the challenges they face in adopting good hygiene habits also suggest that affordability, attitudes, ignorance (in rural areas), and lack of space (in urban areas) are key obstacles to better hygiene and sanitation. Clearly, overall, many households face substantial challenges in benefitting from adequate sanitation. The detailed qualitative analysis provided in chapter 6 provides a richer understanding of the challenges and constraints faced by households in benefitting from adequate sanitation– as well as some of their ongoing efforts to improve water sources in their communities.

Annex 5A: Sanitation and Hand Washing Estimates from the 2011 DHS

Annex 5A.1 Household Sanitation Facilities in the 2011 DHS
Percent

	Households			Population		
	Urban	Rural	Total	Urban	Rural	Total
Improved, not shared facility	20.9	15.3	16.4	26.3	17.4	18.7
Flush/pour flush to piped sewer system	8.6	0.2	1.8	9.4	0.1	1.5
Ventilated improved pit (VIP) latrine	3.7	2.0	2.3	4.8	2.1	2.5
Pit latrine with slab	8.4	12.8	12.0	12.1	14.8	14.4
Composting toilet/Ecosan	0.1	0.3	0.3	0.1	0.4	0.3
Shared facility	51.6	11.3	18.8	43.6	8.0	13.2
Flush/pour flush to piped sewer system	2.7	0.1	0.6	2.0	0.1	0.3
Ventilated improved pit (VIP) latrine	14.9	2.2	4.6	12.3	1.5	3.1
Pit latrine with slab	33.8	8.9	13.5	29.1	6.4	9.7
Composting toilet/Ecosan	0.2	0.1	0.1	0.2	0.1	0.1
Non-improved facility	27.5	73.4	64.8	30.1	74.7	68.1
Pit latrine without slab/open pit	25.2	61.7	54.9	28.0	63.6	58.4
No facility/bush/field	1.8	11.5	9.7	1.8	10.9	9.6
Other	0.5	0.2	0.3	0.2	0.1	0.2
Total	100.0	100.0	100.0	100.0	100.0	100.0
Number	1,691	7,342	9,033	6,468	37,782	44,250

Source: 2011 UDHS survey report.

Table A5.2 Hand Washing in the 2011 DHS
Percent

			Among households where place for hand washing was observed							Number of
	Percentage of households where place for washing hands was observed	Number of households	Soap and water	Water and cleansing agent other than soap only	Water only	Soap but no water	Cleansing agent other than soap only	No water, no soap, no other cleansing agent	Total	households with place for hand washing observed
Residence										
Urban	34.9	1691.0	37.7	0.0	30.0	2.1	0.0	30.2	100.0	589
Rural	27.6	7342.0	23.9	0.5	25.9	3.0	0.7	45.8	100.0	2,026
Region										
Kampala	39.0	797.0	41.7	0.0	30.2	1.2	0.0	26.9	100.0	311
Central 1	50.1	1140.0	45.2	0.0	17.6	3.9	1.2	32.0	100.0	571
Central 2	45.1	1038.0	26.5	0.7	18.1	3.9	1.5	49.4	100.0	468
East Central	30.6	904.0	11.9	0.0	42.9	1.8	0.0	43.3	100.0	277
Eastern	25.2	1226.0	9.3	0.9	29.9	3.2	0.0	56.8	100.0	309
Karamoja	12.5	306.0	1.6	0.0	10.1	0.2	0.0	88.2	100.0	38
North	7.2	757.0	10.3	7.7	19.0	2.3	0.0	60.7	100.0	55
West Nile	16.4	508.0	4.5	1.0	9.9	0.7	0.0	84.0	100.0	84
Western	22.1	1228.0	31.8	0.0	51.1	3.4	0.0	13.7	100.0	272
Southwest	20.5	1128.0	15.6	0.0	22.2	1.8	0.0	60.4	100.0	232

table continues next page

Table A5.2 Hand Washing in the 2011 DHS *(continued)*

Percent

	Percentage of households where place for washing hands was observed	Number of households	Among households where place for hand washing was observed							Number of households with place for hand washing observed
			Soap and water	Water and cleansing agent other than soap only	Water only	Soap but no water	Cleansing agent other than soap only	No water, no soap, no other cleansing agent	Total	
Wealth quintile										
Lowest	17.0	1719.0	11.9	0.8	17.2	0.4	0.8	68.9	100.0	292
Second	23.7	1767.0	12.4	0.8	26.3	3.9	1.0	55.6	100.0	418
Middle	28.5	1672.0	15.0	0.3	31.5	2.5	0.4	50.3	100.0	476
Fourth	32.4	1723.0	26.8	0.4	28.0	2.7	1.0	40.8	100.0	559
Highest	40.4	2152.0	45.7	0.2	27.1	3.4	0.0	23.5	100.0	870
Total	29.0	9033.0	27.0	0.4	26.9	2.8	0.5	42.3	100.0	2,615

Source: 2011 UDHS survey report.

Note: Percentage of households in which the place most often used for washing hands was observed, and among households in which the place for hand washing was observed, percent distribution by availability of water, soap, and other cleansing agents.

References

Alderman, H., L. Elder, A. Goyal, A. Herforth, Y. T. Hoberg, A. Marini, J. Ruel-Bergeron, J. Saavedra, M. Shekar, and S. Tiwari. 2013. *Improving Nutrition through Multisectoral Approaches*. Washington, DC: World Bank.

Barungi, M., and I. Kasirye. 2011. *Cost-effectiveness of Water Interventions: The Case for Public-stand Pipes and Bore-holes in Reducing Diarrhea among Urban Children in Uganda*. Kampala, Uganda: Economic Policy Research Center.

Bbaale, E., and F. Buyinza. 2012. "Micro-Analysis of Mother's Education and Child Mortality: Evidence from Uganda." *Journal of International Development* 24 (S1): S138–58.

Bhutta, Z., T. Ahmet, R. Black, S. Cousens, K. Dewey, E. Giugliani, B. Haider, B. Kirkwood, S. Morris, H. Sachdev, M. Shekar, and the Maternal and Child Undernutrition Study Group. 2008. "What Works? Interventions for Maternal and Child Undernutrition and Survival." *The Lancet* 371 (9610): 417–40.

Cairncross, S., C. Hunt, S. Boisson, K. Bostoen, V. Curtis, I. Fung, and W. Schmidt. 2010. "Water, Sanitation and Hygiene for the Prevention of Diarrhea." *International Journal of Epidemiology* 39 (Suppl. 1): i193–205.

Denboba, A., R. Sayre, Q. Wodon, L. Elder, L. Rawlings, and J. Lombardi. 2014. *Stepping Up Early Childhood Development: Investing in Young Children with High Returns*. Washington, DC: World Bank.

Dillingham, R., and R. L. Guerrant. 2004. "Childhood Stunting: Measuring and Stemming the Staggering Costs of Inadequate Water and Sanitation." *The Lancet* 363 (9403): 94–5.

Esrey, A. 1996. "Water, Waste, and Well-being: A Multi-country Study." *American Journal of Epidemiology* 143 (6): 608.

Esrey, S. A., J. B. Potash, L. Roberts, and C. Shiff. 1991. "Effects of Improved Water Supply and Sanitation on Ascariasis, Diarrhoea, Dracunculiasis, Hookworm Infection, Schistosomiasis, and Trachoma." *Bulletin of the World Health Organization* 69 (5): 609–21.

Fay, M., D. Leipziger, Q. Wodon, and T. Yepes. 2005. "Achieving Child-Health-Related Millennium Development Goals: The Role of Infrastructure." *World Development* 33 (8): 1267–84.

Hutton, G., and L. Haller. 2004. *Evaluation of the Costs and Benefits of Water and Sanitation Improvements at the Global Level.* Geneva: World Health Organization.

Jalan, J., and M. Ravallion. 2003. "Does Piped Water Reduce Diarrhea for Children in Rural India?" *Journal of Econometrics* 112: 153–73.

Kosek, M., C. Bern, and L. R. Guerrant. 2003. "The Global Burden of Diarrheal Disease, as Estimated from Studies Published between 1992 and 2000." *Bulletin of the World Health Organization* 81: 197–204.

Moe, L. C., and D. R. Rheingans. 2006. "Global Challenges in Water, Sanitation and Health." *Journal of Water and Health* 04 (Suppl.): 41–57.

Schuster-Wallace, J. C., I. V. Grover, Z. Adeel, U. Confalonieri, and S. Elliot. 2008. *Safe Water as the Key to Global Health.* Hamilton, Ontario: United Nations University International Network on Water.

Spears, D. 2013. "How Much International Variation in Child Height Can Sanitation Explain?" Policy Research Working Paper No. 6351, World Bank, Washington, DC.

World Bank. 2010. *Water and Development: An Evaluation of World Bank Support, 1997–2007.* Washington, DC: World Bank.

Zwane, A. P., and M. Kremer. 2007. "What Works in Fighting Diarrheal Diseases in Developing Countries? A Critical Review." *World Bank Research Observer* 22 (1): 1–24.

CHAPTER 6

Challenges to Adequate Sanitation: Qualitative Analysis

Clarence Tsimpo, Willy Kagarura, Nakafu Rose Kazibwe,
John Ssenkumba Nsimbe, and Quentin Wodon

Introduction

This chapter complements the quantitative analysis of chapter 5 with a qualitative analysis of some of the challenges and constraints faced by households in benefitting from adequate sanitation—as well as their ongoing efforts to improve sanitation in their dwellings and communities. After a brief description of the methodology adopted for the qualitative fieldwork, the discussion of the data collected through focus groups and key informant interviews is organized along seven thematic issues—the lack of latrines in many household dwellings, the community alternatives to private latrines, the obstacles encountered in building latrines, the incentives that can lead to building more and better latrines, the modes of waste disposal used by households, and the issue of hand washing.

As noted in chapter 5, sanitation can be broadly defined as the set of hygienic means of promoting health and reducing disease through the prevention of human contact with waste hazards. Wastes that can cause health problems for children as well as adults include human and animal feces, solid waste, and domestic wastewater among others. Adequate sanitation has been shown to be essential for a range of development outcomes, including the reduction of diarrheal deaths and the likelihood of malnutrition among young children. Together with access to safe water, adequate sanitation is essential for good health, especially among children.[1] Like access to safe water, adequate sanitation also improves the productivity of workers, not only through better health but also, in some cases, through time savings—having a latrine in one's home is better than having at times to walk a long way to defecate. Apart from improved toilet facilities and proper waste disposal, good hygienic practices such as hand washing with water and soap, or suitable substitutes, are all important part of adequate sanitation facilities and behaviors.

In a similar way to what was done in chapter 4 for the qualitative analysis of access to safe water, this chapter provides an analysis based on focus groups and key informant interviews of some of the constraints encountered in Uganda for improved sanitation. As noted by one of the district water officials interviewed in the fieldwork, formal sanitation coverage statistics may be deceptive and need to be taken with a pinch of salt because the availability in principle in an area of adequate sanitation does not necessary imply that sanitation is indeed adequate in practice. Some areas with comparatively high rates of adequate sanitation as traditionally measured have been recently affected by cholera outbreaks. Many homes do not have rubbish pits or latrines—or when they are available, they may be inadequate—as the district official noted, many people use mosquito nets provided to fight malaria as curtains for their latrines! When public latrines have been made available in communities, schools, or health centers, they may have been poorly managed and maintained, and therefore not be useable.

As noted in chapter 4, there are advantages in combining quantitative and qualitative analysis. General arguments in favor of qualitative work were mentioned in chapter 4 and need not be repeated. But for ease of reference and for readers who may have skipped that chapter, the methodology used for the qualitative data collection is reproduced here from chapter 4.

The qualitative data collection aimed to answer a number of questions emerging from a review of the existing literature and the quantitative (household survey based) analysis of the water and sanitation sector. Some of the questions of interest were as follows: (1) What are the existing perceptions of what constitutes safe and clean water and what practices to improve water quality are undertaken at household level in various regions of Uganda; (2) what are the factors which determine access to safe water for different socioeconomic groups during different seasons of the year and what strategies are adopted to improve access for households?; (3) how has the availability of water for crop and animal husbandry affected people's socioeconomic livelihoods in different parts of Uganda?; (4) what trade-offs are considered in investing in hygienic toilet facilities at the household level and how can we explain the current low percentage of Ugandans who wash their hands with soap after visiting the toilet?; (5) what is the state of the public toilet system in schools, markets, health centers, and places of worship and what factors explain why they are in such a state?; and (6) what are the contrasting practices of wastewater disposal in urban and rural areas and what are the implications and consequences of these practices?

This chapter focuses on the sanitation component of the work. The qualitative fieldwork was undertaken in 14 districts selected in such a way that at least one district was sampled from each geographical subregion of Uganda. In each region, districts were randomly selected from areas with varied water and sanitation performance grading in order to include good, fair, and poor-performing areas in terms of access to safe water in the sample. In addition, purposive targeting was used to select and include districts reflecting some of the main livelihood clusters (pastoralists, crop farmers, fishing) for household. Finally, in each district two communities, one urban and one rural, were visited. The selected districts (as well as their region) for the qualitative fieldwork are shown in table 6.1.

The instruments used for the fieldwork included focus-group discussions (FGDs), key informant interviews, observations, and case studies. Before fieldwork activities, detailed checklists for FGDs and case studies were developed to guide the different categories of targeted populations. The categories of stakeholders that were targeted for data collection included community members (women, men, youth, elderly), leaders of water user committees, local government officials (Chief Administrative Officers or CAOs), district water officers, district health inspectors, district health educators), and, at the national level, officials of National Water and Sewerage Corporation, Ministry of Water and Environment, Ministry of Health officials, and Kampala Divisions Health Inspectors. Some visits to health centres and schools were also conducted to provide a physical assessment of the toilet facilities and provisions for hand washing, with observations and photographs made on site. Visits were also done to water projects like dams and pumping sites.

In what follows, the qualitative data obtained from the fieldwork are organized and discussed along seven thematic issues: the lack of latrines in household dwellings, the alternatives to private latrines, the obstacles to building latrines, the incentives to build latrines, the modes of waste disposal, and finally the practice of hand washing. A conclusion follows.

Lack of Latrines

Many communities have very limited toilet facilities. Consider the case of Paloga in Lamwo district. In that community the subcounty has two toilet blocks: one for staff and the other for the public; but the second one is not in useable state.

Table 6.1 Location of Sampled Districts for Qualitative Research on Water and Sanitation

Region	Districts	Number of districts
Central 1	Sembabule, Kiboga	2
Central 2	Kalangala	1
East Central	Bugiri	1
Eastern	Bukedea	1
Kampala Divisions	Kawempe	1
North/Mid-North	Lamwo, Apac	2
Karamoja/North East	Kotido, Amudat	2
West Nile	Moyo	1
Western/Mid-Western	Masindi	1
South Western	Kisoro, Bundibugyo	2
Total		14

Source: Qualitative fieldwork in this study.

Alongside the two blocks, there is also an old Eco-San toilet that was drainable and separated urine and feces into two separate inlets, but this was abandoned because of poor maintenance. The Health Centre III had a pit latrine block with three stances for men and another three for women, but it was not clean and thereby virtually unusable. The latrine did not have a ramp for people with disabilities because the entry ground is level, but given its lack of cleanliness, it would be too risky to use for people with disabilities. The toilet was about to get full, yet the lengthy bureaucratic procurement process to construct another latrine had not been initiated, so that when full, no toilet would be available at this facility. The district council speaker informed the study team that the district had been constructing drainable toilets at schools and health units, but the draining of the toilets is the responsibility of the school or health unit to which the toilet has been allocated. In his estimation, it costs U Sh 70,000 to pay for one trip of cesspool emptier because they are located in Kitgum and not in Lamwo, which implies an additional charge for the journey from Kitgum to Lamwo.

The only type of toilet available in the community itself was pit latrines, but many households apparently did not have such latrines at home. The lack of latrines is also prevalent in many other communities. In Padibe Town Council, also in Lamwo, no public toilet is available. Lock-up shops and market users, both sellers and buyers, also have no toilet. Most people used the toilet of the Village Local Council Chairman, who had, out of kindness, granted free access. Since close to 1,000 people come daily from the three surrounding subcounties to this market, either to sell or buy various food items, a lack of toilet could be a potential health disaster.

In Moyo Town Council, there are three public toilets. One of them charges U Sh 300 per use, but it was reported that many try to evade paying. At the public toilets, water for hand washing is available, but soap is not provided. One of the public toilets is manned by a volunteer and has a room set aside for people with disabilities. A problem mentioned was that the public toilets are locked at night. In addition, more public toilets will need to be constructed to accommodate the expanding population. There is also a public toilet at Moyo Stadium, but it is not useable because no one has looked after it. It apparently belongs to the Education department, but it has not discharged the responsibility of ensuring that it is maintained. The Town Council in principle has flush toilets, but there are not actually functioning because piped water is only available for two hours per day. In lodges and hotels, some of the water systems are in place as well, but also not working efficiently because of inadequate provision of piped water.

In Town West village in Moyo, there are two public toilets. One was constructed by the subcounty local government and was supposed to be looked after by the Beach Management Unit. But it has been used badly, especially at night, and is not in a useable state. Its doors were stolen. Some fishermen come and use the toilet at night. When they find it locked, they climb its sheltering wall and squat on its top and defecate. Most of the homes near the beach do not have toilets, and residents want to use the subcounty toilet without paying. The community proposed that the subcounty deploys a guard to look after the public toilet, anticipating that this person would collect money from those using the toilet so that it could be maintained. The second toilet was constructed by the Uganda National Roads Authority for passengers of the public ferry that passengers use to cross the river Nile. This second toilet has a user charge of U Sh 100 and is very clean in comparison to the one constructed by the subcounty.

Among all districts visited, Kotido has the lowest latrine coverage at 18 percent (the national average is 64 percent), but this is an improvement versus the coverage of 3 percent five years earlier. This improvement resulted from sensitization campaigns, but as a district official explained, *"The toilets we have in Kotido are not even the standard latrines that you find in other regions; here we only have some structures resembling toilets."* In Karamoja, one of the poorest areas in the country, when households must choose between food and latrines, the latter becomes a luxury. As a resident exclaimed: *"What shall we deposit in those toilets you are telling us to build in a situation where we do not have food to eat?"* In the urban center of Kotido Town there are two public toilets, one at the car park and the second one at the market where people are charged U Sh 100 per visit. But few people go there because they are not accustomed to toilet use, let alone having to pay for it. A nongovernmental organization (NGO) constructed a public toilet in each of the wards of the Town Center, but its contract ended, and they handed over the toilets which are full.

Some areas have better latrine coverage. In Kiboga town, most houses have a toilet. One exception is the house of a temporary worker who comes and goes away frequently. Three types of toilet facility are encountered in the community. The first type consists of pit latrines 40 feet deep covered with a slab and with walls made of bricks, roofed with iron sheets, and sheltered by a wall. Most do not have doors because of termites that destroy the wood. This is the most common type in this community. The second type consists of pit latrine covered with a slab with walls made of bricks and cement, a door for privacy, roofed with iron sheets, and sheltered by a wall. The third type consists of pit latrines covered with poles on the floor, with walls made of mud and wattle roofed with iron sheets and no door. Because of the dangers of not having toilets, community members think that stringent rules should be in place to ensure that all households have a toilet. Participants also agreed that if local governments were empowered to conduct effective sensitization and grass root training, noncompliance would be reduced.

In Ishondoro, Kisoro district, most facilities are traditional pit latrines with about 6–10 feet in depth because of the soft soil that lead people to avoid digging deeper since pits could collapse inwards. Only the well-to-do and a few centers in the community (health centers and some schools) have latrines made of bricks, cement, and iron sheets. Households without toilets use open defecation in bushes or toilets from neighbors. Some people have been caught digging pits but not real latrines as a disguise for authorities in order to get around strict byelaws. Finally, water officers also pointed out that pit latrines are not well suited for some urban areas where space is limited to locate latrines and smell carries to neighbors.

Therefore, it was suggested that in those areas people build drainable toilets instead, or simple flush toilets which drain into a pit (aqua privy technology), but this does not seem to have been popularized in the communities yet.

In Kalangala Rural, latrines are communally shared, which contributes to a lack of cleanliness because of lack of proper ownership and incentives for maintenance. There were no byelaws on latrine construction since communal latrines are the ones present in the area. Because of the collapsible nature of soils, toilets cannot be deeper than 15 feet. But because of shoddy work, all the toilets constructed by the district collapsed and community members must now contribute for the construction of new latrines, with each adult person asked to contribute U Sh 10,000.

In some fast-growing areas such as Kyatiri village in Masindi district, quality latrines are available in schools and health centres. The majority of the residents have temporary and semi-permanent latrines made of local materials such as mud, wattle, and grass (as well as timber when available). Yet, many households are without latrines and the area is becoming crowded with limited space to allow for latrine construction. This leads latrines to be shared, typically by about five families. Incidences of open defecation are quite common. Part of the lack of latrines is attributed to poor planning in this upcoming town that does not allow adequate construction since plots are sold haphazardly and demarcated without following required standards (probably in part because of corruption). The space is further limited by an inflow of migrants. Finally, cost constraints are also highlighted here as elsewhere as being a hindrance. To redress the issue of limited latrine coverage, respondents in focus groups suggested that the government should come in and help in supplementing people with portable shrubs since local materials for construction such as timber no longer exist because of a high level of deforestation in the community.

Alternatives to Private Latrines

The first alternative to private latrines is the availability of public toilets, often with an associated fee for their use. In Kalangala Town Council, for example, those without latrines use district office facilities during the day. At night some use toilet facilities at the market, while others defecate in bushes. Community members contend that with public toilets the use of bushes and littering of feces would be reduced. In many communities, public toilets were considered as a good alternative. They should have a caretaker to ensure that they are clean. They should be located in a place convenient to everyone, and not in a place where others notice you going to the toilet. The public toilets should have running water and soap and, if possible, separate stances or rooms for women and men. Charging fees helps for maintenance and cleanliness.

Short of the use of public latrines when households do not have private latrines, other options are unfortunately inadequate. Some households that have no latrine and do not want to pay fees for using public latrines simply rely on the latrines of neighbors, which can create tension and conflict in the community. In Village Inn Cell, people without toilets go to those of their neighbors, with or without their permission. Some even went to the extent of breaking the padlocks on these toilets whenever they found them locked, and accordingly, most residents had given up the practice of locking the toilets because they have had to buy padlocks to replace those broken. In Masindi Town, some use the latrines of others (not necessarily with permission again), while others use *buvera* (polythene bags) at night and dispose the matter in garbage bins.

The option of open defecation has its own risks and burdens. A person has to wait until it is safest and no one is seeing him, most often at night; one has to go to a different place each time so as to confuse those who would take a keen interest in one's movements; the possibility of snake bites is real in the bushes where open defecation is often done; the shame and humiliation if one is discovered to be indulging in open defecation is a big cost in the community; the fact that the bush grass needs to be bent down for one to defecate, and as one leaves, this grass bends upwards and smears the person as he goes away must also be taken into account; and above all, the disease one is spreading through open defecation are a cost for all.

In the Karamoja region in Moyo District, toilet coverage is low. In order to avoid cholera associated with flies, residents there have a system of killing some donkeys and leaving them in the fields, so that the flies remain on the rotting donkeys and do not go to their Manyatta homesteads. Urine and the blood of donkeys are also believed to have antiseptic qualities.

Obstacles to Building Latrines

There is near unanimous appreciation in communities of the danger of not having latrines and the risks this generates in terms of disease outbreaks. It was also pointed out that welcoming and entertaining visitors became very embarrassing if the home had no toilet. In Lamwo, residents considered that *"an ideal toilet facility is a pit latrine with a roof, door, hand washing facility (we use ash for hand washing here), a clean smeared floor (we use cow dung and cannot afford cement slabs for toilet floor). Some of the floors of our latrine pits are wooden, over which we put polythene and cover this with soil. A good latrine can be used for 5 years."* In Apac, community members enumerated what they considered the characteristics of a good latrine: It must be located 30 meters away from the main house, it must have a cover for the lid/hole to stop flies and bad smell from contaminating the environment; it must have provision for hand washing, or alternatively ash can be used to clean fingers after using the toilet; it needs to have old newspapers as toilet paper, or soft leaves from nearby bushes to serve the same purpose; it must have a door for privacy; it must have a roof so that it can be used in bad weather; it must have a cement slab or a floor smeared with cow dung and black soil to enhance cleanliness.

Yet, while community members agree on what a good latrine should be, many residents still did not have latrines of their own in their home. Cost is one factor.

In Apac, the estimated cost for constructing the ideal pit latrine was estimated at U Sh 7 million. Such costs are beyond the means of many. In Kotido as well, in Karamoja district (one of the poorest areas in the country), the town clerk informed the study team that constructing a decent toilet requires U Sh 6 million, beyond what the poor can afford. In that area, there is also no lagoon where sewage could be treated, even if some might have been able to connect to a sewage system.

At the same time, why do many have mobile phones but no toilet? When asked this question, community members provided an array of interesting answers. A mobile phone can be given to you by a friend or relative, but a toilet cannot be donated like this. A mobile phone is much cheaper than constructing a toilet. Mobile phones may cost as little as U Sh 30,000 and you cannot construct a toilet facility at that amount. A person can even acquire a mobile phone by stealing it from others. In one village, local council leaders were given mobile phones free of charge by the ruling National Resistance Movement party during the last elections in 2011. Mobile phone is also a sign of modernity. When you do not own a mobile phone, people take you as backward, one elderly man explained, adding, *"That's why you find a home with 5 mobile phones with no toilet facility."* A mobile phone is also useful, with many functions other than communication. Many of the phones have radios, torches, clocks, and calendars, so people find them more sophisticated and more useful than the construction of toilet facilities.

In addition to cost, other factors were mentioned for the lack of latrine in many homes. Some people are too old or have physical disabilities which prevent them from digging pits, while others were abducted, tortured, and weakened during the 20-year Lord's Resistance Army insurgency, and were also not physically able to dig and construct their latrines. And while many claim not to have the money to pay those who dig latrine pits, some residents were also considered by the communities as just stubborn and negligent not to build latrines.

In Nakaperimolu, a congested conglomeration of fenced clusters of manyatta homesteads, only pit latrines with grass thatched roofs are available. There is a house for civil servants but it also has no toilet. Community members said they need cement slabs because termites eat the wood used for latrine floors. The texture of the soil is bad and toilets sink in frequently. Above all, the settlement pattern is such that there is no space within the enclosure to locate a toilet. Participants in focus groups were quite conscious of the dangers of not having a toilet, citing their role in preventing disease spread and reducing water contamination. The main issue on public toilets was a plea that they must be cost free because people will not be able to find the money to pay. As there are many homes without toilets, people go with a hoe and defecate in holes and bury it. Others said they had not time and money to construct a toilet. Here, digging the toilet is men's work, so women are helpless when men do not construct the toilet.

Town West village in Moyo is a community with many fishermen, fish mongers, retail businesspeople, and peasants. A public toilet is paid for by users. While many homes have pit latrines with proper or temporary shelter, an estimate 40 percent have no toilets, in part because of construction issues. The soil texture is reportedly brittle and may sink into pits. The water table is high and digging pits may not be an option. The village suffered from a cholera outbreak, and two factors were mentioned by residents as its lead causes. One was the slope of the landscape. Under heavy rains filthy water is washed downwards and settles near the village. The second factor is the soil texture which, as mentioned, crumbles and leads toilets to cave in with their entire shelters. A different type of construction is needed to overcome these challenges.

In addition, many residents in Town West village are migrants who are renting houses for short durations—they consider it the responsibility of landlords to provide toilets: *"We are migrants to a village located near the lake. We expect the land owners, whose houses we are renting, to construct the toilets, and not ourselves. But some landlords ask us to construct the toilets, yet we are here for a very temporary time span. Fishing, the main activity of our livelihood, is seasonal and we keep moving to different locations from time to time."* The settlement pattern is also such that households are squeezed with limited space for constructing latrines: *"We had a conflict in our area from 1986 to 1998 and many people came here and concentrated in places which they considered safe. When the conflict ended, many people refused to move back to those communities from which they had come. Yet there is very limited space here for everyone to find a place to locate a pit latrine in this community."* And the cost of constructing a good pit latrine is high, as in other communities. Still, some residents are simply considered negligent and do not respond to fines imposed on homes without toilets. As they try to use others' toilets for free, the few who have toilets resort to padlocks to avoid trespassers.

The issue of the responsibility of tenants and landlords was also raised in Kampala where respondents suggested that the Kampala Capital City Authority should close houses without toilets. Some community members proposed however that loans for building toilets should be given to the poor. But many suggested that the presence of many rented tenements created a pervasive *"I don't care attitude,"* with the area dominated by tenants seeking low transportation and housing costs and newly arrived residents said to have poor cultural attitudes toward good hygiene.

One option considered in some communities where latrines can easily sink in and collapse as result of poor soil texture is to use other materials, such as timber and bamboo for construction. This also reduced the cost of latrines in comparison to using bricks and cement. However, the risk when using timber and bamboo for construction is that such latrines cannot last for long because of termites that destroy timber and wood. In some areas it was also noted that because of the soil profile, people cannot dig a pit that goes beyond six feet in depth. These complications and cost concerns lead some communities to construct grass-thatched toilets with walls made of mud and wattle that may be below the required standards within the town council.

In some areas, landownership is also an obstacle to the construction of latrines. In one of the communities without a single public toilet, focus-group participants explained that no one was willing to offer land where the public latrine could be located. It was also noted that where public toilets were constructed, they were taken over by landowners after being vandalized by the public. They then ceased being public toilets. To respondents in that community, public toilets should be free especially those in market places since market vendors already pay taxes. Such public toilets should be the responsibility of the Town Council since its mandate is to manage and safeguard cleanliness in public places. As one respondent argued: *"It is useless to pay for public toilets because that money is not accounted for."* But without fees of some sort, it is very difficult to operate and maintain public toilets in a sustainable manner.

In some areas such as Amudat district, cultural factors also play a role in the lack of latrines. It is tradition that one should never see one's spouse answering nature's call. People take toilets as an imposition from outsiders, which they vow to resist. The chief administrative officer wanted to start a campaign to at least ensure that people use hoes to bury feces. He also proposed that if latrines are constructed at those places where herdsmen water their animals, this may be a good entry point into initiating behavior change to embrace the use of toilets. But people insisted that this would violate the secrecy that is supposed to be observed. In Kangaror Cell within Amudat Town Council, community members again insisted that toilets are a foreign imposition to their culture. Even if this were not so, there are, as elsewhere, financial costs involved in constructing toilets, and people prioritize access to food and water first, with toilets far down their priority list. Installing public toilets with fees is not an option there.

As a community member in Amudat district explained: *"I cannot use the money that I would have used for salt and divert it to pay for visiting a toilet. We have survived for a very long time with open defecation. Long ago, we did not develop the practice of using toilets because we are nomadic and were always on the move. Toilets are a permanent structure for those who have gone to school. We believe that those who have never produced children will become barren if they use the toilet. Toilets are too dirty and they can contaminate us instead of helping us stop the spread of disease."* People were well aware of the costs and risks of open defecation, and they cited the following: snake bites, scorpion bites, sharp poisonous thorns which prick people and they develop abscesses, as well as infestation with worms. Still one member reiterated, *"We need to guard secrecy so that no one sees us as do open defecation."* Another told the meeting, *"We cannot go with a hoe, because the secrecy will be broken when people see us carrying hoes, and we are herd men mainly, not crop farmers."*

Cultural and lifestyle obstacles to latrines were also mentioned in Sembabule town, where the way of life of Bahima cattle keepers contributes to some households not having toilets. These are nomadic people who keep moving from place to place in search of pastures and water for their animals. Therefore, constructing permanent houses and pit latrines appears to them as being a waste of time. At the same time, those sentiments appear to be fading away gradually.

Incentives to Build Latrines

What can be done to encourage households to build pit latrines? Information provided to households can help. In most districts, before allocating a water point to a community, a baseline survey is undertaken, with the meeting used as an opportunity to communicate the importance of each home having a toilet and of locating toilets far from water sources. Home inspections can also help. The Moyo district has launched a campaign for all homes to have a toilet. Existing toilets tend to be pit latrines that are too small in size (a person cannot turn around once inside). Leaders have asked community members to build pits for latrines at least 15 feet deep. In Apac, the district water officer drew an historical contrast between past and current standards of domestic health inspection. *"In the 1970s Health Assistants used to visit homes to assess and guide on domestic hygiene and sanitation, particularly to ensure there was a toilet facility in every home, and that it is located appropriately from the place where food was prepared and cooked. I much wish that this role could be revived,"* he nostalgically reminisced. The idea to rejuvenate home inspection visits by health assistants and enforce laws mandating latrines was mentioned in other communities as well. In addition, an elderly man explained: *"Government giving assistance to persons with disabilities and the elderly though local governments would also help in ensuring that all homes in the community have toilet facilities. Many elderly and those with disabilities have toilet facilities in bad condition or do not have toilets at all."*

Enforcement of fines, byelaws, and rules is another option. Some communities suggested that those without latrines in their home should be brought to the police and made to dig a toilet at a health facility or a school as a way of making them able to appreciate that they could indeed dig a latrine pit in their home if they put their mind to it. In Moyo, the District Council has approved byelaws on water and sanitation. The first people to be arrested for not having toilets in their homes have been local village leaders, to help set an example and try to change attitudes. Under the byelaws, health assistants also have to sign a certificate of approval of all new toilets.

Unfortunately, while most local governments have byelaws on sanitation and water for homes and businesses, they are often not enforced in part because politicians do not want to annoy voters and interfere with the technocrats who are charged with enforcing the laws. As a respondent exclaimed, *"even Museni can make laws but find them not operational."* As a woman further explained, *"there are sanctions against people without latrine; since most people are tenants, landlords are supposed to provide their tenants with a pit latrine, a compost pit for waste management and a soak pit on their bathrooms. Failure to comply leads to a warning with a grace period of two weeks to do the needful. Failure to submit then should lead to be taken to the municipality authorities or the court. However due to some political interferences and fear for hatred, leaders have failed to make these sanctions and by-laws functional and effective."*

A more effective action suggested by some communities is to make access to government programs conditional on having a toilet in one's home. In Atopi village, Apac, all homes in the village were reported to have a latrine. The homes were visited by members of the Village Health Team, and households without a toilet were fined U Sh 5,000 and asked as a formal written undertaking to build a toilet in a specified time frame. In that community, a latrine in the home is also a condition to access government programs such as those provided by the National Agricultural Advisory Services (NAADS). In Apac town, leaders reportedly made regular inspections and closed business premises with hygienic conditions below acceptable standards.

In some communities, apart from efforts to enforce regulations on private latrines, social pressure is used to encourage all residents to construct latrines. In Bugiri, community members are required to sign an undertaking in writing that they will observe proper hygiene by having a toilet and adopting other good practices. This has led to high toilet coverage. But even here, the sanitation coverage looks impressive, but it constantly shifts from time to time. In the rainy season, many toilets collapse and sink in, yet to have a community free of open defecation must rely on use of local materials, which are temporary. There has also been an attempt to use the Public Health Act to charge some extreme cases in the courts. Another measure has been the use of shaming those without toilet facilities at public meetings, but this may affect negatively some among the poorest who may not have the means to actually afford the construction of latrines.

Another alternative to encourage latrines in the home is to charge fees at public latrines. Apac town has four types of toilets: flush toilets, VIP toilets, pit latrines, and Eco-San toilets. The fee to use public toilets is U Sh 100 (such fees were accepted in many communities because they help for the maintenance of the public toilets, which are placed where the density of the population is high, including near eating houses and markets and bars). Yet, despite such fees many homes still do not have toilets, apparently for four main reasons. First, the area is in a swampy location where the water table is so low on one side of the town that constructing pit latrines there is expensive. Second, the area is densely populated. The limited space is a constraint to construct toilets since people only have very small plots of land. Third, when toilets are full it is expensive to empty them using cesspool trucks that cost U Sh 120,000 per trip. Finally, the pattern of settlements is such that these trucks do not have clearly designated ways to reach the latrines that need to be emptied, which reduces the incentives to build them.

Finally, a note is warranted about Eco-San toilets that have been introduced in many areas. Most people do not like them for several reasons: They need climbing to enter them, they are expensive, and they are cumbersome to empty regularly. The toilets have proved difficult to manage. One block constructed at Moyo Technical Institute fell out of use because it was not managed sustainably.

In Kamwokya Kifumbira, a slum surbub of Kampala, few latrines are available, and those that exist are only five to ten feet deep. Eco-San toilets were constructed by an NGO, but did not work well in the community because of overpopulation and mismanagement. Eco-San toilets are complicated to use because they require the separation of urine and feces. They also require a dry cleaning material such as ash. But Muslims do not like to use a toilet arrangement that does not provide for water, and in some areas it is cultural taboo to put ashes on feces. In Nakaperimolu, community members declared Eco-San toilets to be for educated people.

Waste Disposal

Improved sanitation is not only a matter of latrines—it also requires proper waste removal. As mentioned previously, most communities visited for the qualitative fieldwork have a good understanding of what good sanitation and hygiene practices require, but they are not always able to observe such practices. Households know that apart from a clean toilet facility with a cover, proper sanitation requires ideally a rubbish pit for depositing solid waste, a drying rack for household utensils, a hand-washing facility to wash hands after visiting the toilet, slashing around the home, a separate house for domestic animals, a kitchen where food is prepared and cooked, and a soak pit to dispose of wastewater. In addition, personal-level good hygienic practices mentioned by respondents included bathing daily, brushing one's teeth, washing one's clothes, shaving, and putting on ironed clothes. As a woman explained it, *"When one talks about sanitation, my understanding is having a toilet in good condition, bath shelter, drying rack, kitchen, a refuse bin, a separate house for animals and being able to boil water. Then on my body I am supposed to brush my teeth and clean my body."*

In the case of waste disposal, when describing their actual practices, many respondents especially in rural areas agreed that there is no single system followed. Many local governments do not have specific regulations, so households do what is convenient for them. Households with enough space to dig compost pits and deposit solid waste there (which is then used as manure in gardens) do so, while others may simply drop waste in gardens before decomposing. Households with little land may burn solid waste while others may litter waste on pathways.

In urban settings, waste disposal tends to be regulated, with private garbage collectors picking up waste for a fee while publicly provided waste disposal is limited to public settings and some residential areas. In Kawempe, for example, *"private garbage collectors come in and offer their services at a negotiable price to different communities within the division, while KCCA garbage collection is limited to schools, commercial premises, institutions, and all fenced bungalows."* Waste burning is not allowed in urban settings because of the fire risks and pollution it creates for other dwellings nearby. Laws are however not well enforced and followed, and in many areas lack of access roads means that garbage trucks cannot reach

Water and Sanitation in Uganda • http://dx.doi.org/10.1596/978-1-4648-0711-4

many households—those who do not benefit from garbage service may simply drop rubbish in water channels alongside the roads: *"Most dispose of rubbish in gardens. Waste water is also poured in the surrounding bush or gardens. But even in civilized Kampala the disposal of waste water and rubbish is like what we do in our village! There is no organized waste water disposal."*

Ideas are being tried to improve waste management. As for latrines, sensitization and information campaigns can help. In Sembabule, a district official explained, *"Home improvement campaigns have also been put in place by the district. In these campaigns, education and persuasion are made in order to make sure that most of the communities without latrines comply. Besides, other sanitation components of an ideal home state for example a drying rack, refusal pits, kitchen and bathroom are re-emphasized during these campaigns."* In Moyo, a district officer explained, *"Central government provided a tractor for urban waste management. Because the site for recycling has not been developed yet, the tractor has not yet been used, but in the next financial year, the first phase of developing the recycling site will be done with fencing and dust bins. The Town Council also has 16 casual laborers who collect rubbish from households and take it on wheel barrows to where it is burnt."* In a few areas, with support from NGOs waste disposal was well organized with bins and compartments for organic and inorganic refuse, so that *"waste management is no longer a problem."*

When some households do not practice sound waste management, the community can retaliate, using some of the same mechanisms as those mentioned in the case of latrines. A respondent in Atopi Village explained that *"the sanction on sanitation and hygiene is by community members blacklisting you and not even drinking water from your home is you get known to be dirty and unhygienic."* Communities can also impose financial sanctions. In Kalangala District, an official explained that *"the town council has sanctions for violating established sanitation practices. Health assistants move in the community, warning households and if one is defiant he/she is taken to court and a fine of 50,000 or punishment through community service is given. Sometimes places of businesses (restaurants and bars) are closed."* In Kampala, garbage trucks are in place and private collectors have been given the mandate to collect (at a fee) garbage in areas not reached by trucks. People have been made aware of steep fines levied against those caught dumping waste in unlawful areas or open spaces.

Yet, on financial sanctions, a common view is that while sanctions exist, they often do not serve their purpose because of the leaders' negligence and at times corruption. As a respondent put it: *"The sanctions set for solid waste management and waste water are not effective since no one has ever been penalized as a result of mismanagement by the leaders."* A similar argument emerged from key informant in other areas: *"The Chief Administrative Office introduced an ordinance to improve sanitation in the district, but it has faced stiff resistance in the district council, and it has stalled there. The leaders themselves are reluctant to change from traditional behaviors and they have resisted compulsory penalties for non-compliance with good hygiene."*

In addition, in many cases resources are lacking to remove waste. Some Town Councils have no funds to buy trucks. In others, available equipment may be failing in disrepair. As noted in a community with trucks: *"On the resource part, each truck is apportioned 35 liters of fuel on a daily basis by the head office and it is support to collect garbage for 14 routes. But this is at times impossible due to fact that some trucks end up breaking down given their dilapidated state while other vehicles are shared with the engineering department and are sometimes taken on for road and drainage repairs."* Lack of repair was also mentioned for tractors: *"Sanitation is a very big challenge. We received a tractor, but its trailer got spoilt and was taken to Kampala for repair. It has been there for one year and we do not know what is happening to it."* Finally, apart from lack of resources, late payments are also an issue in some communities: *"We received a tractor for transporting garbage and a tipper lorry for repair of roads. Garbage collection and disposal is tendered out to a private contractor. But this contractor is not paid promptly and is currently owed 40 million Shillings. He struggles to get the district to pay him."*

Hand Washing

The last topic on which the qualitative fieldwork focused was that of hand washing, which is also part of the required hygiene to avoid the spread of disease. Unfortunately, in some areas, hand washing appears to be the exception rather than the rule. Apart from cost and availability of water or facilities to wash hands, lack of knowledge about the potential consequences of not washing hands plays a substantial role in the lack of take-up for the practice in quite a few of the communities visited (and more so apparently than in the case of water and sanitation).

In Kalangala Rural, hand washing was not common. The communal toilets did not have facilities for hand washing because of lack of attendants. In Kalangala Town Council, community members agreed to the importance of hand washing, especially after visiting the toilet, but they also reported that a big percentage of community members did not actually practice it, and this could be due in part to a lack of information. One middle-aged woman said: *"When campaigns and trainings on hand washing are done, many of the community members do not attend them, saying that these trainings are a waste of time. Even the trainings are few and are mainly concentrated on the main land. The campaigns are rare in the far away islands."* In Sembabule town, hand washing was also found not to be a common practice, and those who washed hands hardly ever used soap. Lack of knowledge and awareness of the potential consequences of not washing hands after a toilet visit was again mentioned as a probable cause.

In Bumadu in Bundibugyo district, the issue of handing washing seemed to be known and understood as important to one's health. Yet again, relatively few households followed the practice. One of the main reasons mentioned for not practicing hand washing was that some passersby steel the soap and containers reserved for that. Others said that the cost of soap and containers limited the practice. In Kiboga as well, hand washing was relatively rarely practiced, and the two reasons advanced by community members were ignorance (many households do not know the dangers that come with not washing hands after visiting the toilet) and scarcity of water (some households that were actively practicing hand washing gave up because of that scarcity). In addition, as a woman explained, *"We used to have hand washing utensils but the children would play with them and waste the water, so we gave up with the practice."* In Moyo as well, it was mentioned that when soap would be available some children removed it for their games.

In Kamonyi, Kisoro town, participants agreed that most people know in principle about the need to wash hands, but only a handful do it. To members, this was evidence that there is still lack of knowledge, inadequate sensitization, and negligence that require more efforts from authorities. In Ishondoro, Kisoro Rural, while participants were again aware about the importance of hand washing, they did not do it systematically and not with soap because soap is reserved for critical domestic uses such as bathing and washing clothes and utensils. Yet, others refuted this idea, saying that hand washing with soap is not put into practice because of people's negligence as according to them there are always some small pieces of soap left after washing and bathing in every home. Participants proposed more home-based training and sensitization campaigns so hand washing gains acceptability and becomes an integral aspect of domestic hygiene.

The same was observed in Kijjura, Masindi urban, where despite awareness of hand washing, the practice had not yet been adopted widely. Whenever there is a cholera outbreak, members practice it for a while, but the practice dries up soon after. In addition, for those who try to wash the hands at the facility near the public latrine, soap is often missing because it has been stolen. Even metallic jerry cans are stolen by those involved in scrap collection and sale. The issue of the soap and jerry cans being stolen was also mentioned in Kagango. Others noted that they were constrained by the little money they had and could not afford to buy the containers where water for hand washing can be kept. But for this case, it was almost unanimously agreed that very few households could justifiably cite this as their real hindrance in that community. In other communities, however, cost may be a real issue. In northern Uganda in Paloga, Lamwo district, the lack of hand washing was blamed on cost as money was lacking to buy water containers and soap.

In Kyaimba, Kiboga district, some people mentioned that *"people are disrespectful to leaders whose messages champion hand washing."* There is a need for more intensive sensitization in order for the population to adopt this culture. In Apac district as well, the community views on hand washing underlined soap as expensive to provide regularly for this purpose. But they also noted as a key underlying constraint the fact that people in their community had not been brought up in the culture of hand washing right in the homes where they are raised. In their view, therefore, it still required massive sensitization to be adopted.

In Moyo, disaster presented opportunity for behavior change with respect of hand washing. The deputy chief administrative officer noted that a recent outbreak of cholera led to four deaths and 142 cases of admission. A massive mobilization of community members on hand washing was carried. As a result, by the time of the fieldwork all district and subcounty offices had a hand-washing facility at the entrance, complete with soap and jik (a detergent). Compulsory hand washing had also been implemented at the River Nile crossing points for all passengers who use the ferry to cross. But even there it was observed that the challenge of hand washing is that it needed to be learnt when young, rather than adopting the practice only when an outbreak of disease erupts. All the same, the scare of the disease significantly helped to make people adopt the practice, since the danger was seen as very real. It was such a matter of life and death that people decided to wash their hands before they entered their houses after being away for some time, so as to avoid bringing in the cholera from wherever they would have travelled.

The issue of leadership was also emphasized as critical in Moyo. At an inter-district meeting held in Nebbi in May 2014, all leaders committed themselves to ensuring that all homes in the districts of West Nile would have VIP toilets with clean surroundings, and to enforcing hand washing using small jerry cans. This was in recognition and response to the fact that many people had toilets, yet sanitation-related and waterborne diseases continued to rise. The biggest challenge on hand washing was said to be the fact that it had not been inculcated right from childhood. Availability of water and affordability of soap were also noted as occasional constraints. An additional constraint noted there was the fact that responsibility in the home is not allocated to ensure that regular refills of water at the hand-washing facility whenever it is used up. So when someone finds the water used up, she/he walks away without washing hands.

In Bugiri Town Council, tip taps for hand washing exist, but it was remarked that many were for show for the health assistants who inspect homes. After they leave, no one bothers to effectively use the hand-washing facilities. The general attitude is that hand washing is not a very important aspect of hygiene. Again, children were noted to divert the tip taps for their games. It was also observed that some schools could not afford decent hand washing because of the large number of students they have. In Bugiri Rural, it was noted that Muslims had permanent small jerry cans for hand washing, but they did not necessarily use soap, which led to the comment that jerry cans alone may transmit germs from the toilets when soap is not used.

Overall, apart from issues of cost and stolen soaps, it is clear that more sensitization and leadership is needed to achieve higher rates of hand washing in the communities. As a district official summarized it very well: "*Local leaders have campaigned, but there is poor response and adoption, because hand washing is viewed as a very strange practice to the local culture in which people have not been exposed to it since childhood. In ordinary circumstances, soap is expensive to community members and water is quite scarce. Most significantly, local leaders themselves are not visibly seen practicing hand washing, even at the high district level. Yet people are like children, who copy what they see. You cannot simply continue telling people about what they should do, but do not see you doing, and hope to have them buy your idea.*"

Conclusion

This chapter provided a qualitative analysis of some of the challenges and constraints faced by households in benefitting from adequate sanitation—as well as some of their ongoing efforts to improve sanitation in their dwellings and their communities. After a brief description of the methodology adopted for the qualitative fieldwork, the discussion of the data collected through focus groups and key informant interviews was organized along seven thematic issues: the lack of latrines in many household dwellings, the community alternatives to private latrines, the obstacles encountered in building latrines, the incentives that can lead to building more and better latrines, the modes of waste disposal used by households, and the issue of hand washing.

The qualitative fieldwork suggests that many communities have limited toilet facilities, with quite a few of the latrines built in a state of disrepair, especially for public facilities. Private latrines are not affordable for many. Yet, apart from cost, other obstacles including poor soil quality, lack of land rights, tenant status, and even cultural traditions all may come in the way of better sanitation. Alternatives to public or private latrine are many, but often inadequate, because unsafe. When public latrines are available, there is often a consensus that in order to ensure proper maintenance, fees should be charged to those using the latrines, yet enforcing the fees requires leadership in the community that is at times lacking. The same is true for byelaws stating, especially in urban areas, that households should build their own latrines—often enforcement of these laws is weak. Information campaigns can help in building consensus at the local level of the need for better sanitation. Some communities condition access to government programs on having a proper latrine in the home. In some areas, home inspections are organized to certify the presence latrines. Even shaming has been used in some communities to incentivize households to build proper latrines. Technological alternatives such as Eco-San toilets have also been proposed, but these are often not seen favorably by households, and also fall in disrepair.

Beyond latrines, improved sanitation requires proper waste removal. Most communities and households are again well aware of what should in principle be done, but some of the same constraints are at work to limit the ability of households to properly dispose of waste. When local governments do not have specific regulations, households may simply do what is convenient for them. In cities, garbage disposal is in principle, but not necessarily in practice, better organized. Burning is often not allowed because of fire risks and pollution, but enforcement may be limited. As for latrines, sensitization and information campaigns can help, and when some households do not practice sound waste management, the community can retaliate using some of the same mechanisms as those mentioned in the case of latrines, but this again requires leadership.

A special focus was placed on the practice of hand washing, which remains the exception as opposed to the rule. The issue of cost is again prevalent, for example to buy the necessary containers and soap—some of which may be stolen at public facilities that do not have tight oversight. But in this specific case, lack of knowledge about the benefits of hand washing seems to be a larger issue. In one community, the threat of a cholera outbreak led members to wash hands for a while, but the practice dried up soon after. Overall, as was already observed for the analysis of access to safe water, leadership and perseverance at the local level appear to be both required for implementing solutions that are often context- and community specific.

Note

1. There is a very large literature on the links between water and sanitation on the one hand and health on the other (see among many others Alderman et al. 2013; Bhutta, Ahmet, and Black 2008; Cairncross, Hunt, and Boisson 2010; Dillingham and Guerrant, 2004; Esrey, 1996; Esrey et al. 1991; Fay et al. 2005; Hutton and Haller 2004; Jalan and Ravallion 2003; Kosek, Bern, and Guerrant 2003; Moe and Rheingans 2006; Rijsberman and Zwane 2012; Schuster-Wallace et al. 2008; Spears 2013; World Bank 2010; Zwane and Kremer 2007; and finally Denboba et al. 2014 in the context of early childhood).

References

Alderman, H., L. Elder, A. Goyal, A. Herforth, Y. T. Hoberg, A. Marini, J. Ruel-Bergeron, J. Saavedra, M. Shekar, and S. Tiwari. 2013. *Improving Nutrition through Multisectoral Approaches*. Washington, DC: World Bank.

Bhutta, Z., T. Ahmet, R. Black, S. Cousens, K. Dewey, E. Giugliani, B. Haider, B. Kirkwood, S. Morris, H Sachdev, M. Shekar, and the Maternal and Child Undernutrition Study Group. 2008. "What Works? Interventions for Maternal and Child Undernutrition and Survival." *The Lancet* 371 (9610): 417–40.

Cairncross, S., C. Hunt, S. Boisson, K. Bostoen, V. Curtis, I. CH Fung, and W.-P. Schmidt. 2010. "Water, Sanitation and Hygiene for the Prevention of Diarrhea." *International Journal of Epidemiology* 39 (Suppl. 1): i193–205.

Denboba, A., R. Sayre, Q. Wodon, L. Elder, L. Rawlings, and J. Lombardi. 2014. *Stepping Up Early Childhood Development: Investing in Young Children with High Returns*. Washington, DC: World Bank.

Dillingham, R., and R. L. Guerrant. 2004. "Childhood Stunting: Measuring and Stemming the Staggering Costs of Inadequate Water and Sanitation." *Lancet* 363 (9403): 94–5.

Esrey, A. 1996. "Water, Waste, and Well-Being: A Multi-country Study." *American Journal of Epidimiology* 143 (6): 608.

Esrey, S. A., J. B. Potash, L. Roberts, and C. Shiff. 1991. "Effects of Improved Water Supply and Sanitation on Ascariasis, Diarrhoea, Dracunculiasis, Hookworm Infection, Schistosomiasis, and Trachoma." *Bulletin of the World Health Organization* 69 (5): 609–21.

Fay, M., D. Leipziger, Q. Wodon, and T. Yepes.2005. "Achieving Child-Health-Related Millennium Development Goals: The Role of Infrastructure." *World Development* 33 (8): 1267–84.

Hutton, G., and L. Haller. 2004. *Evaluation of the Costs and Benefits of Water and Sanitation Improvements at the Global Level*. Geneva: World Health Organization.

Jalan, J., and M. Ravallion. 2003. "Does Piped Water Reduce Diarrhea for Children in Rural India?" *Journal of Econometrics* 112: 153–73.

Kosek, M., C. Bern, and L. R. Guerrant. 2003. "The Global Burden of Diarrheal Disease, as Estimated from Studies Published between 1992 and 2000." *Bulletin of the World Health Organization* 81: 197–204.

Moe, L. C., and D. R. Rheingans. 2006. "Global Challenges in Water, Sanitation and Health." *Journal of Water and Health* 04 (Suppl.): 41–57.

Rijsberman, F., and A. P. Zwane. 2012." Copenhagen Consensus 2012 Challenge Paper: Water and Sanitation." http://www.copenhagenconsensus.com.

Schuster-Wallace, J. C., I. V. Grover, Z. Adeel, U. Confalonieri, and S. Elliot. 2008. *Safe Water as the Key to Global Health.* Hamilton, Ontario: United Nations University International Network on Water.

Spears, D. 2013. "How Much International Variation in Child Height Can Sanitation Explain?" Policy Research Working Paper No. 6351, World Bank, Washington, DC.

World Bank. 2010. *Water and Development: An Evaluation of World Bank Support, 1997–2007.* Washington, DC: World Bank.

Zwane, A. P., and M. Kremer. 2007. "What Works in Fighting Diarrheal Diseases in Developing Countries? A Critical Review." *World Bank Research Observer* 22 (1): 1–24.

PART 3

Policy

CHAPTER 7

Public Funding and Programs for the Poor in Water and Sanitation

Samuel Mutono, Elizabeth Kleemeier, and Fredrick Tumusiime

Introduction

This chapter complements the diagnostic of previous chapters by analyzing trends in public funding for the water and sanitation sector and some of the main initiatives implemented over the last decade in order to better serve the poor. The analysis suggests that public funding for the sector has increased in real terms but remains low in comparison to needs. Even though some of the schemes implemented under the 2006 pro-poor strategy have been successful, access remains low and rural households remain at a disadvantage versus urban dwellers. It is important to take stock of what has been achieved, and what remains to be done to improve access and affordability for the poor.

Nearly a decade ago, the Directorate of Water Development (DWD) in the Ministry of Water and Environment (MWE) issued a pro-poor strategy to guide activities within the DWD mandate. The 2006 DWD *Pro-Poor Strategy for the Water and Sanitation Sector* has never been reviewed in its entirety, despite plans to do so after two years. The objective of this chapter is to take stock of the extent to which the water and sanitation sector has been given priority in budget allocations and discuss some of pro-poor initiatives in the sector in order to inform future policy.

The 2006 strategy covered areas of the water and sanitation sector within the mandates of DWD and the National Water and Sewerage Corporation (NWSC). Responsibility for implementing the strategy was given to DWD and NWSC (and sub-entities with these two organizations). This explains why sanitation and hygiene promotion receive little attention in the strategy as these activities fall largely under the purview of the Ministry of Health (MOH) and Ministry of Education and Sports (MOES). It also explains why off-farm use of water for productive purposes and water resource management activities were included in the strategy, along with drinking water supply. The strategy was short (ten pages long), and it comprised 36 strategic actions, including cross-cutting issues such as budget allocation and monitoring. Although the actions in the strategy were specific, they were not stated in a way that was clearly measurable, nor were there targets or milestones against which to evaluate progress. There was also no plan for monitoring and reporting on the strategy's implementation and achievements. The intention was that these facets of monitoring would be developed as part of the strategy's implementation, but the extent to which this happened turned out to be limited.

The objective of this chapter is to complement the diagnostic of previous chapters by assessing trends in public funding for the water and sanitation sector and reviewing some of the initiatives implemented over the last decade to better serve the poor. Section 2 is devoted to an assessment of trends in public funding for the sector. Section 3 considers some of the main schemes implemented under the pro-poor strategy to serve the poor. A brief conclusion follows.

Level of Public Funding

Public funding for the social sectors, which include water and sanitation, has been declining over the last decade in Uganda. While the social sectors commanded between 35 percent and 40 percent of the budget up to 2002/03, this declined to under 30 percent by 2011/12. Meanwhile, the budget share of the economic and productive sectors has risen from 10 percent to over 35 percent. Within the social sectors, funding for the water and environment sector has increased, but this is more the case in terms of allocations than actual disbursements. In constant 2003 prices, the budget for the water and sanitation sector increased from UGx 68 billion to UGx 158 billion. As shown in figure 7.1, the gains in terms of released funds have been lower. Between 2008/09 and 2012/13, there has been an increase expenditure in real terms, but this increase remains limited with a stagnation in funding over the last few years.

While funding has increased in recent years, the levels of funding provided remain well below needs identified in the Sector Strategic Investment Plan (SSIP). These shortfalls may indicate that the SSIP was fiscally unrealistic in light of available resources. However, the investment plan seems to represent a credible estimate of the fiscal resources that would be necessary to achieve the goals for the sector. Table 7.1 compares the level of resources actually allocated to those that would be needed, confirming large gaps between both, especially in rural areas (in urban areas, both "on-" and "off"-budget funds are considered; off-budget funds are provided mostly in terms of what can actually be tracked through NWSC).[1]

Figure 7.1 Water and Environment Sector Budget, Released Funds, and Expenditures

UGx billions in constant 2003 prices

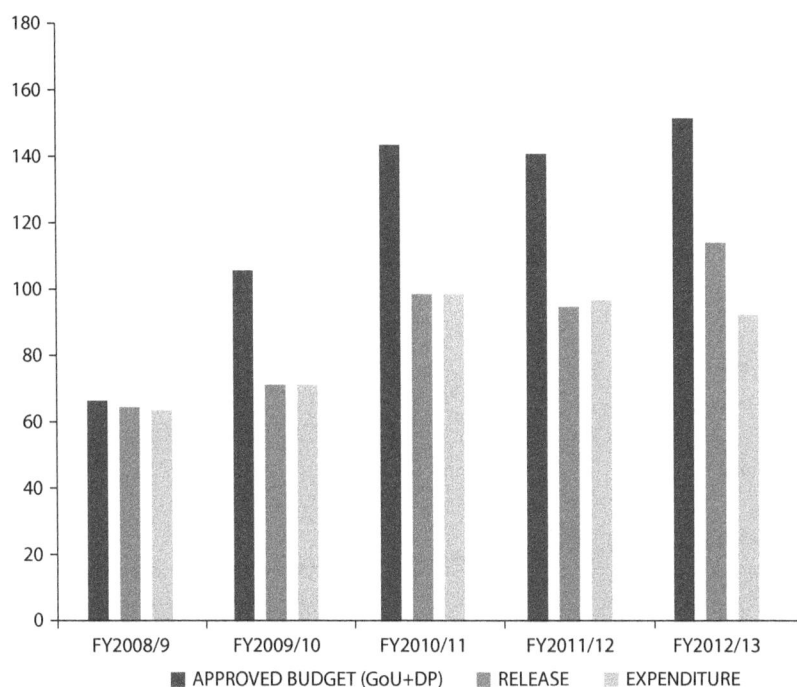

■ APPROVED BUDGET (GoU+DP)   ■ RELEASE   ▨ EXPENDITURE

Source: Government data.

Note: Figures include both government and donor funds.

Table 7.1 Released and Required Funds to Achieve Targets

UGx billions, nominal

Sub-sectors	2009/10	2010/11	2011/12	2012/13
Rural Water Supply and Sanitation				
SSIP rural water	89	119	144	172
Released funds, on-budget	71	72	72	52
Released Funds as Percentage of SSIP	*80*	*61*	*50*	*30*
Urban Water Supply and Sanitation				
SSIP urban water and sewerage	85	80	118	128
Released funds, on-budget	45	30	34	73
Released funds, off-budget for NWSC concessional grants and loans	—	18	17	4
Released Funds On- and Off Budget as Percentage of SSIP	*—*	*60%*	*43%*	*60%*
Off-budget, NWSC internal revenue	—	24	19	5
NGO Off-Budget, Released Funds	**19**	**18**	**42**	**32**

Source: Calculations from database maintained by MWE.

Note: MWE = Ministry of Water and the Environment; NWSC = National Water and Sewerage Corporation; NGO = nongovernmental organization; SSIP = Strategic Sector Investment Plan. — = not available.

Table 7.2 Share of Released Funds for Water Supply and Sanitation Subsectors
Percent

Sub-sectors	2009/10	2010/11	2011/12	2012/13
Shares (on-budget funding only)				
Rural water and sanitation	46	51	51	34
Urban water and sanitation	29	21	24	48
Water for production	15	15	15	11
Water resources management	9	13	10	7
Shares (including off-budget NWSC funding)				
Rural water and sanitation	—	45	45	33
Urban water and sanitation	—	30	32	49
Water for production	—	13	9	7
Water resources management	—	12	9	7

Source: Calculations from database maintained by MWE.
Note: — = not available.

There also seems to have been a recent shift in the allocation of funds between urban and rural areas, as shown in table 7.2. The share of funding allocated to rural water and sanitation used to be at about half of on-budget spending between 2009/10 and 2011/12, but this dropped to one-third in 2012/13. If off-budget funding for NWSC through concessional grants and loans is included in the analysis, the share of funds allocated to rural areas is even slightly lower. This therefore begs the question as to whether funding is allocated in priority to reach the poor, most of whom continue to reside in rural areas today.

Another indicator of lack of necessary funding relates to funding provided to district water offices (DWOs), which shoulder the main responsibility for rural water supply services. District Water and Sanitation Conditional Grant (DWSCGs) are central grants to district offices which account for about a fourth of the water and sanitation budget. These grants represent a declining share of the overall water and sanitation budget, and as a result have been declining in real terms as shown in figure 7.2. The decline in DWSCGs has been accompanied by the need to use more of these funds to establish DWOs in the newly created districts. Williamson et al. (2014) mention the importance of sustaining and building the capacity of local government departments to provide services. Yet, this has also meant that funds available for actually expanding rural water access have declined even more over time in rural areas.

Targeting the Poor

The previous section suggests that while funding for water and sanitation has increased in real terms, in comparison to other sectors, this increase has been modest. In addition, funding for rural areas, and especially DWOs, has been declining. This is a source of concern for a pro-poor strategy. A number of initiatives that

Figure 7.2 Released District Water and Sanitation Conditional Grants

UGx billions, nominal and constant 2003 prices, 2002/03–2013/14

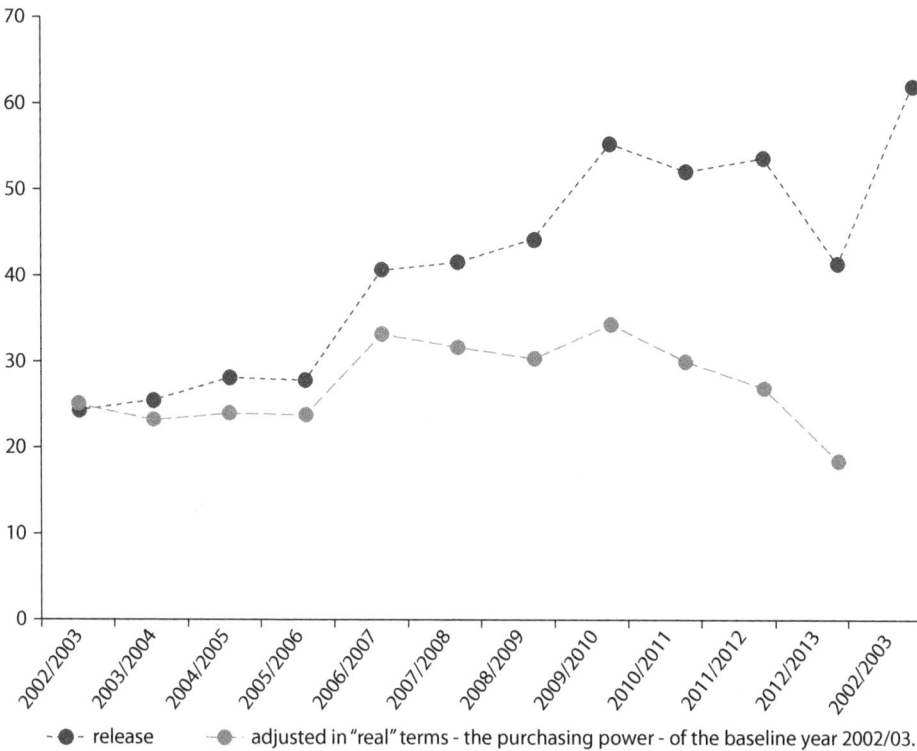

- ● - release   - ● - adjusted in "real" terms - the purchasing power - of the baseline year 2002/03.

Source: Mulders (2015) based on Ministry of Water and Environment data.

could in principle be pro-poor have been undertaken in the water and sanitation sector in recent years. This section reviews a subset of those initiatives to provide a partial assessment as to whether they are likely to have succeeded.

Rural Areas

One of the actions recommended by the 2006 pro-poor strategy was to empower communities through participation and to ensure cross-subsidies in cost recovery. On the question of empowerment, a survey commissioned by the ministry looked at community participation throughout the project cycle for water and sanitation projects (Asingwire 2011). Results from 160 water supply projects suggest low levels of participation, particularly with respect to the choice of the technology used in the project. The survey did provide some evidence of cross-subsidies since interviews with water committee members suggested that some vulnerable groups were exempted from operation and maintenance contributions (see table 7.3). At the same time, most people continue to not contribute enough to operation and maintenance, which reduces the importance of the findings in that those not belonging to exempted vulnerable groups also do not contribute

Table 7.3 Exemptions from Cost Recovery by Village Water Committees

Group reportedly exempt from contribution	Percentage of responses citing group (%)
Elderly	79
Persons with disability	53
Very poor	15
Widows and child-headed households	12

Source: Asingwire 2011.

very much. Bey et al. (2014) looked at the issue question in 16 sub-counties in 8 districts in northern and western Uganda. They found that whether or not people contribute to operation and maintenance varies across districts. The Asingwire (2011) study attributes low contributions to people's reluctance to contribute unless the project infrastructure had actually broken down, as well as to perceptions of poor management by village water user committees. The Bey et al. (2014) study reached similar conclusions. Overall, this suggests that the water supply projects in rural areas are likely to have achieved mixed success only.

Another way to target the poor is through allocations to districts that have high poverty rates. Formulas are in place to determine how much funding districts should receive under DWSCGs, but this does not carry further to particular subcounties. Sectorial guidelines indicate that 65 percent of funds should go to subcounties, and 70 percent of the funds should be spent on rural water supply. Yet, local politicians can and do override the technical and equity recommendations of DWOs in order to allocate more funds to often better-served district. Fund allocations based on access rates also do not target the poor specifically, and previous analysis of the relationship between poverty and access rates in rural sub-counties suggests weak correlations. Furthermore, even targeting funds to the poorest districts does not necessarily reach the poorest households and people. First, districts that are not particularly poor may have pockets of poverty. Second, when a poor district receives funds, it does not automatically follow that the poorest areas will be funded. In 2009, DWD and Uganda Bureau of Statistics (UBOS) collaborated in developing a planning methodology to address drawbacks in the allocation of funds on the basis of access rates (DWD 2009). The report does not advocate focusing only on poverty in allocating funds. Rather, the argument is that poverty should be used as a criterion along with cost, efficiency, and equity. The report goes on to make a number of more specific recommendations as to how to make this happen, but the methodology was never implemented.

Urban Areas

NWSC manages the water networks in Kampala and 29 towns and municipalities. In small towns outside NWSC's mandate, the water supply is generally managed by local water authorities under the authority of the ministry. There are currently 157 small towns, 105 of which had piped schemes. Note that the number of "large towns" increases regularly, as DWD and NWSC agree to transfer responsibility to NWSC for growing town networks. The main programs for the poor are (1) tariff subsidies; (2) reduced connection fees; (3) other types of public water points, (PWPs) including shared yard connections and authorized water vending; and (4) investments in additional pipelines and PWPs in low-income settlements.

Tariff subsidies are embedded in tariff structures that set some or all tariff rates below operating costs. Examples of subsidized tariffs include the fact that NWSC sets lower tariff rates for PWPs and shared yard connections than for other types of domestic connections, as well as institutional, government, industrial, and commercial connections. NWSC charges the same tariff in all large towns, thereby providing a subsidy to those consumers in towns that have above average operating costs. In 2012/13, 25 out of 80 small town schemes did not cover their operating costs implying that tariffs were implicitly subsidized in those towns (Tsimpo and Wodon 2017a, see also Tsimpo and Wodon 2017b for an analysis of the water and sanitation sector using data from Uganda's household surveys). Another form of tariff subsidy (not used in Uganda) is an increasing block tariff, in which the rate per cubic meter depends on how much water the connection holder consumes. For example, a household that consumes 10 cubic meters per month would pay at a higher rate than a household consuming under 6 cubic meters in a month. Recent World Bank research in Uganda indicates that most tariff subsidies benefit primarily wealthier households. Tsimpo and Wodon (2017a) found that for households with a piped connection in their dwelling, the wealthiest 30 percent of the population would capture 66.2 percent of the benefits from any of the simulated subsidies in their models for Ugandan tariffs, including increasing block tariffs. The bottom 40 percent would receive just 12.5 percent of the benefits, and the poor would receive none of the subsidies.

Tariffs subsidies benefit the wealthy because so few among the poor have access to piped schemes. Tsimpo and Wodon suggest that connection subsidies would be more effective than tariff subsidies in delivering piped scheme benefits to the less wealthy. These findings with respect to both tariff and connections subsidies are in line with an earlier World Bank global study on utility subsidies and the poor (Komives et al. 2005). Similar findings come from an analysis of the impact of NWSC pro-poor policies (WSP 2013). An analysis of NWSC 2010 data for large towns (see table 7.4) shows that house and yard connection users received most of the subsidy, and the households that have such connections tend to be better off than those that do not.

Another way to provide services to the poor consists in lowering the fees for a domestic connection and introducing installment plans for paying the fees. Such measures have worked in other African countries (Komives et al. 2005). In 2004, NWSC issued an Affordable Connections policy to reduce connection costs (fee plus other costs) for all consumers. The objectives were to increase the number of connections (particularly among the urban poor), reduce the

Table 7.4 Allocation of Subsidies, by Connection Type, Large Towns, 2010

Connection Type	Average tariff	Total subsidy (U Sh)		
		Total	Per connection	Per capita
PWPs	1,214	3,058,131,641	394,699	2,631
Yard and house	1,981	14,166,016,880	68,319	10,295
Institutional/government	3,241	(6,299,741,581)	(1,112,243)	
Industrial/commercial	3,508	(10,924,406,940)	(403,293)	

Source: WSP 2013, pg. 54, based on data from NWSC Annual Report, 2009/10.
Notes: PWPs exclude shared yard connections and includes kiosks. Yard and house includes shared yard connections, which are virtual PWPs. Average tariff is calculated by dividing the total revenue for each category of connection by the volume billed. Thus, the average includes various service charges. The above figures may overestimate the per capita subsidy to yard and house connections. The per capital subsidy is calculated on the assumption of 150 persons per PWP and 6.6 persons per yard and house connection.

level of nonrevenue water, and ensure the quality of materials used in connection service lines. Under this policy, the cost to the consumer for a standard household connection or yard connection was cut from U Sh 125,000 (USD 75) to U Sh 59,000 (USD 35), with NWSC constructing and paying costs for the service line from the water main to the consumer's meter within 50 meters of the main. This last provision saved consumers something on the order of USD 200–300, an even more significant source of savings than the reduced connection fee. For customers located more than 50 meters from the main, the customer would pay half the costs of installing the service line. Maintenance and repair of the service lines to the consumers' meters also became NWSC's responsibility. Reconnection fees were reduced to U Sh 75,000 (USD 45). To fund this policy, NWSC imposed a 10.7 percent surcharge on the tariffs to all consumers, domestic and otherwise, with the intention to ring-fence these monies in a fund devoted to new connections (WSP 2013).

The policy outperformed expectations in Kampala in that new connections increased at an annual average of 14,500 after 2004, compared to the 7,000 annual average before 2004. The demand for new connections was actually even higher than this, but NWSC imposed annually a ceiling of 10,000 to 15,000 new connections, given limits on piped water production and transmission capacity and the additional work created for operations (billing, revenue collection, pipeline maintenance and repair, connection installation). As a result, water supply coverage, as estimated by NWSC, grew substantially between 2002/03 and 2010. Most (77 percent) of the new connections in Kampala were domestic, that is, yard and house, and most of these new residential connections were for house connections. The policy significantly raised revenue for NWSC thanks to an increase in new customers, the additional tariff surcharge, and subsequent yearly tariff increases in line with sector price indices and inflation. Operational costs also more than doubled in 2004–10, but revenue consistently represented around 130 percent of operating costs, excellent performance by international benchmarks for this ratio. However, because coverage at the household level remains low even in Kampala, where poverty rates are also lower, it is not clear whether this policy benefitted the poor, strictly speaking.

In small towns, WSDFs commonly offer subsidized connections for a short period during the construction phase as a promotion. Offered on a first-come/first-served basis, 50–100 connections are made available for around U Sh 50,000 compared to an actual cost of approximately U Sh 300,000. The demand for subsidized connections far outstrips the available financing. After construction, Umbrella Organizations for Water and Sanitation (UOWS) may provide meters and materials to provide additional subsidized connections. Limited funding necessarily constrains the extent of this. According to the DWD database on small town and rural growth center schemes, 27 schemes offered a subsidy on new connections at some point after commissioning. But the subsidies were only available for a few months in total for each participating scheme.

A third pro-poor practice has been to introduce lower cost alternatives to house connections for domestic customers. The alternatives differ in their physical design and location, their expected use and management, and sometimes their tariffs, but a common alternative consists in expanding PWPs and Yard Taps in large towns. WSP (2013) provides figures on the number of new yard connections and PWPs provided in 117 designated poor areas of Kampala between 1998 and 2011. In total, 14,668 yard connections and 1,530 PWPs were provided. These investments have clearly expanded access to water for the poor. But one problem facing service through yard connections and PWPs has been disconnection for nonpayment. In 2010, the 21 percent of new yard connections were inactive, and this was the case for half of PWPs. In recent years, NWSC has been able to reduce the number and proportion of inactive connections through better planning for PWPs and the activities of the Pro-Poor Unit (for example, socioeconomic surveys, consumer education). However, it is difficult to see the impact of these activities in reducing inactive connections, because long-inactive connections are eventually written off the books. Other impediments to increasing the number of PWPs in Kampala's poor settlements have been the limited number of pipelines in these areas, and the unavailability of suitable land.

To meet the challenges facing PWPs and shared yard connections, particularly nonpayment, NWSC has piloted 300 prepaid PWPs in Kampala. The advantages to the consumer are in principle 24/7 water availability at the point and no middleman mark-up in price. For NWSC, prepayment helps in eliminating nonpayment. The challenges are the much higher costs of installation (about USD 1,350 compared to USD 380 for a PWP and USD 170 for a yard connection), repairs and maintenance to the meters and vendor machines that charge the tokens, and continuing problems of locating available land. Still, the pilot experience has been sufficiently positive to approve a larger project that will expand the model substantially.

One urban action in the 2006 pro-poor strategy involved establishing authorized water vending. The concept is to permit and encourage domestic connection holders to resell water to their neighbors at the same tariff established for

PWPs. These authorized vendors would be allowed to keep a percentage of the tariff as a profit. NWSC has implemented a similar concept through shared yard taps. The utility uses meter readings to identify yard connections that are operating as virtual PWPs, verifies this situation through field visits, and then applies a lower tariff. This approach avoids the problem of having households apply for connections with the special tariff and then using the water mostly for themselves. Small town schemes offer yard connections, and the general assumption is that water reselling takes place at nearly all of these taps to some extent. However, data are lacking to assess how successful the schemes have been. The challenge is how to prevent the resellers from marking up the price to as much as the market will bear, and capturing the subsidy for themselves. The upward market pressures on prices can be substantial in small town schemes, whose production may be far lower than demand.

Finally, NWSC, particularly in Kampala, has expanded pipelines in low-income settlements. Concessional funding has gone into both projects targeted at expanding the network in low-income Kampala settlements and in expanding production capacity to supply the system. Still, the amount of water available has constrained network expansion and new connections. Small town schemes have different challenges. Unlike in Kampala, the low-income households may not be concentrated in separate settlements, but instead may live interspersed with higher-income households. Piped schemes in small towns are designed to serve the densely populated areas, often the town centers, in order to keep the investment and operation and maintenance costs at an affordable level. A densely populated rural area adjacent to the small town boundary is more likely to be served before a less densely populated area within the small town's administrative boundaries. These practices are in line with piped scheme design guidelines, good engineering practice, but may again have a limited reach to some of the poorer households. The issue is that extending pipelines to serve low-income households does not make economic or engineering sense if the poor live in less densely populated and scattered parts of small towns.

There are also some risks involved. Piped schemes serving certain parts of small towns can lead to worse water services in other parts. Towns with piped schemes have been gazetted, and the responsibility for water services turned over to a local water authority (typically a Water Supply and Sewerage Board). At this point, the district council is no longer directly responsible for water services, and the DWO ceases to construct or maintain the boreholes, or use the District Conditional Water and Sanitation Grant within the town limits. Meanwhile, WSDFs concentrate their funds on piped schemes serving a portion of the town's population, with no responsibility to improve water services through other means for those people outside the piped scheme supply area. The water authority has to take over financial and technical responsibility for improved sources outside the supply area yet within the town. Information is not available on whether in practice local water authorities have been able to maintain or increase town water services both inside and outside the piped scheme supply areas.

Conclusions

Efforts have been made in Uganda to provide water and sanitation supply to the poor in both urban and rural areas. Public funding for water and sanitation has increased in real terms over the last decade, but remains low in comparison to needs. Some of the schemes implemented under the 2006 pro-poor strategy have been successful in expanding access, but access remains low, and to a large extent the needs of urban dwellers have been served more than those of the rural poor. Almost ten years after the 2006 pro-poor strategy, it is now important to take stock of what has been achieved, and what remains to be done to promote access and affordability for the poor. It is hoped that the diagnostic provided in this study will be helpful for that purpose.

Note

1. "On-budget" funds refer to donor and government funds that are incorporated in the government's budgeting system. "Off-budget" funds refer mainly to donor funds that continue to disburse outside government systems, through direct disbursement to NGOs, NWSC, or projects. MWE has figures for off-budget funds for NWSC and NGOs. However, the NGO figures are not complete and are not broken down by subsector, and therefore cannot be included in the budget breakdowns in this section.

References

Asingwire, N. 2011. *Assessment of the Effectiveness of the Community-based Maintenance System for Rural Water Supply Facilities*. Kampala: Ministry of Water and Environment.

Bey, V.,P. Magara, and J. Abisa. 2014. *Assessment of the Performance of the Service Delivery Model for Point Sources in Uganda*. The Hague: IRC.

DWD. 2009. *Strategic Investment Plan for the Water and Sanitation Sub-Sector*. Kampala: Government of Uganda.

Komives, K., V. Foster, J. Halpern, and Q. Wodon. 2005. *Water, Electricity, and the Poor: Who Benefits from Utility Subsidies?* Washington, DC: World Bank.

Mulders, C. 2015. *Trends in Funding to the Water and Environment sector in Uganda over Last Five Years*. Kampala: Water and Sanitation Sub-Sector Development Partners Group.

Tsimpo, C., and Q. Wodon, eds. 2017a. *Residential Piped Water in Uganda*. Washington, DC: World Bank.

Tsimpo, C., and Q. Wodon, eds. 2017b. *Water and Sanitation in Uganda*. Washington, DC: World Bank.

Water and Sanitation Program. 2013. *Do Pro-poor Policies Increase Water Coverage? An Analysis of Service Delivery in Kampala's Informal Settlements*. Washington, DC: World Bank.

Williamson, T., et al. 2014. *Review of Budget Support to Uganda 1998–2012*. London: Overseas Development Institute.